ROSEMARY DRYSDALE
SEED STITCH

beyond knit 1, purl 1

sixth&springbooks | NEW YORK

Library of Congress Cataloging-in-Publication Data is available upon request

MANUFACTURED IN CHINA

1 3 5 7 9 10 8 6 4 2

First Edition

 sixth&springbooks

104 W 27th St, 3rd Floor,
New York, NY 10001
www.sixthandspring.com

"Ribbing, moss, seed, and garter are all balanced and combine the yin and yang of knitting."
–STEPHANIE PEARL-MCPHEE

contents

84

86

88

94

98

100

102

116

118

120

122

130

134

introduction

I was born and grew up on the northeastern coast of England, close to many
fishing villages. I would see the fishwives there sitting outside their cottages, selling
fish and wearing their handknitted shawls. They also knitted nonstop, hardly
ever looking at the work. The fishermen wore their navy blue handknitted
gansies with yokes decorated with seed stitch patterns.

The first thing I remember knitting is a pair of socks on double-pointed needles. (I use "pair" loosely, since I may have only completed one sock at the time.) I was probably eight years old. I do not remember learning pattern stitches, such as cables, until much later. I originally learned how to knit in the round, and only worked purl stitches when turning the heel of a sock.

When I did start working different pattern stitches, I was inspired by my love of the colorful Fair Isle patterns from Scotland and the simple fishermen's sweaters from the Channel Islands, but I was mostly drawn to the graphic look of seed stitch (known to us in the UK as moss stitch) and cables on Irish sweaters with their clean, crisp lines.

This book developed from my love of graphic seed stitch patterns and the beautiful colors in Fair Isle knitting. I've worked out more than 50 different pattern stitches that use seed stitch—some use only one color, but most use two colors or, in some cases, three. I had a great deal of fun creating these patterns, using only the knit stitch and the purl stitch (though some yarn overs do creep in!). I hope you will enjoy this book as much as I've enjoyed bringing it to you and that you'll develop a love of the versatile, beautiful, classic seed stitch.

KNITTING AND PURLING: A BRIEF HISTORY

No one can be sure when in human history knitting began, or how it came about. Examples of a form of knitting have been found in Egyptian tombs, and fragments of sandal socks were discovered knitted by the nomadic tribes of Arabia, who could carry their work with them from place to place. Most early pieces of knitting were worked in the round, using a number of double-pointed needles. Stockings were the most common items made, out of silk, often using many colors worked in decorative patterns. At this time knitted items were exclusively made for royalty and the rich.

Until the early sixteenth century, the knit stitch was the only stitch used. Working in the round with every round knitted produced the "stockinette stitch" pattern.

Purl stitches first appeared in the mid-sixteenth century, incorporated into a pair of red silk stockings knitted for Eleonora di Toledo, wife of Cosimo de Medici. Stockings then were worked in either silk or cotton, with very fine threads and a gauge of as many as 25 stitches per inch. Purl stitches may have been used earlier than this in the turning of the heels of socks, though no samples have been found. When both knit and purl stitches were used in the work, either in isolated units or in groups, the results were decorative patterns representing the effects of woven damask. An excellent example of this technique, resembling a brocade pattern, is found in the garment knitted for King Charles.

Why was it called the purl stitch? Maybe because the little bumps made by the purl stitches represented beads, or "pearls." In work knitted flat, alternating one knitted row with one purled row—a technique that also developed around the sixteenth century—the knit side of the work was sometimes called the plain side, and the bumpy side (or opposite side) was called the purl side. Of course, depending on the design, either side of this fabric could be referred to as the right side, but more often it was the plain side, or flat side.

During the seventeenth and eighteenth centuries, knitting was no longer only for the rich. The people of the Scottish Isles made sweaters, socks, gloves, and hats for personal use and also for sale. The fishermen's sweaters had brocade-like yokes worked with seed stitch patterns on stockinette stitch backgrounds. Each knitter had his or her own designs and worked from memory. On the Aran Isles on the west coast of Ireland, fishermen wore similar sweaters to those in the Scottish Isles, traditionally called "ganseys." The name is derived from Guernsey, one of the Channel Islands. Another commonly used name is "jerseys," after the other Channel Island, Jersey.

By the nineteenth century, flat knitting had become very popular, and knitting pins, similar to the knitting needles used today, were made in many different sizes. In the twentieth century, Irish knitters started working cable patterns into the fishermen's sweaters, and this distinguished them from the Scottish gansey. Often these cabled garments are referred to as Aran sweaters. Seed stitch and moss stitch were combined in various ways with the cables, and the resulting patterns were given descriptive names such as marriage lines, tree of life, waves, and flags.

This is only a brief overview of the history of the knit and purl stitch. For more details on the history of knitting, I suggest "The Sweater Curse" by Alison Lurie, published in *The New Yorker* magazine on August 28, 2013. It is fascinating reading for anyone interested in knitting. ■

the anatomy of seed stitch

Seed stitch is made up of knit stitches and purl stitches. These can be arranged in many ways to produce interesting and beautiful **patterns, as** seen in the swatches on pages 16–77.

Seed stitch can be worked over an even number or odd number of stitches. I prefer an odd number. When working over an even number of stitches, the first stitch is a knit stitch and the next stitch is a purl, and this is repeated across the row, ending with a purl stitch. This is usually written in a pattern as:

ROW 1 *K1, p1; rep from * to end.

The next row calls for knitting the purl stitches and purling the knit stitches, and is usually written as:

ROW 2 *P1, k1; rep from * to end.

These two rows are repeated to form the pattern.

Here's an easy way to remember how to "knit the purl stitches and purl the knit stitches": If the next stitch to be worked is a knit stitch, it will look like a "V," and you will purl this stitch. If the next stitch to be worked is a purl stitch, it will look like a bump, and you will knit this stitch.

On the other hand, when seed stitch is worked over an odd number of stitches, you will always knit the first stitch and purl the next stitch and repeat this across the row, ending with a knit stitch. This one row is repeated every time you turn the work, and is usually written as:

ROW 1 K1, *p1, k1; rep from * to end.

I find that for a knitter just learning seed stitch, working over an odd number of stitches is easier, as you do not have to think about knitting a purl stitch or purling a knit stitch, or worry about whether you're on the right or wrong side of the work.

To avoid confusion, keep in mind that in British knitting patterns, seed stitch is called moss stitch, or single moss stitch, maybe because it resembles the moss grown on the stones all over Britain. If working from a British pattern, "moss stitch" should be worked as American seed stitch. The pattern that is called moss stitch in the U.S. (which is a four-row repeat, see page 18) is different from the British moss stitch—which is called double moss stitch in the UK.

Seed stitch patterns have many advantages: often they are

8

reversible, which is ideal for scarves, open cardigans, and blankets. They have a firm, heavy texture, making a great fabric for outergarments; for example, Irish knit sweaters incorporate many seed stitch patterns for extra thickness and warmth. The patterns lie flat, so the edges will not curl and need very little blocking—a small border of seed stitch on each side of a stockinette stitch piece stops the work from curling. As there are only two stitches involved, the knit and the purl, a beginner knitter can easily master the seed stitch pattern.

SEED STITCH IN THE ROUND
When we knit in the round, the right side of the work is always facing, so it's clear to see whether each stitch is a knit or a purl. Whenever possible, seed stitch in the round works best with an odd number of stitches on the needle. Place a marker at the beginning of the round and start with a knit stitch, then a purl stitch, and repeat these two steps (k1, p1) around. You will end the round with a k1, then slip the marker and begin the next round p1, k1, continuing to alternate around. It's that simple!

If there has to be an even number of stitches on the needle, you will begin round 1 with a knit stitch and end the round with a purl stitch. However, on round 2, you will begin with a purl stitch—making two consecutive purl stitches, one at the end of the first round and one at the beginning of the second round.

On round 3, you will be faced with two consecutive knit stitches. At the end of each round you will work a knit stitch or a purl stitch, and the automatic reaction would be to make the next stitch the opposite. Resist this instinct! If you end with a knit, the next round will begin with a knit. You must take care at the beginning of the round when working with an even number of stitches, and it will also result in a pattern that's not as perfect as you might like, so try whenever possible to have an odd number of stitches.

INCREASING IN SEED STITCH
Increasing (adding stitches) is used to shape a piece of knitting. Many kinds of increases can be used when working seed stitch—practice some to see which produces your favorite finished result. (I've used the abbreviation M1 to indicate increases in this section.) My preferred method is to knit (or purl) into the front and back of the stitch. When increasing in seed stitch, the aim is to keep the pattern correct. Before you add a new stitch, first look at the second stitch on the needle. If it is a purl, you have to increase by purling into the front of the first stitch, then knitting into the back of the same stitch. If the second stitch is a knit stitch, increase by knitting into the front of the first stitch and then purling into the back. This will maintain the pattern of alternating knit and purl stitches.

It is easier at the end of the row: just continue in the pattern, knitting or purling the increase into the last stitch. For example, if the last stitch is a knit stitch, you will purl into the front and knit into the back of the stitch.

INCREASE STITCH PATTERN

15 sts inc'd to 19

STITCH KEY

⊟ p on RS, k on WS   Ⓟ M1P

▨ no stitch

INCREASING IN THE MIDDLE OF A FLAT PIECE OF WORK
The increases are worked at either side of a knit stitch. (beginning with 15 sts)
ROWS 1 AND 3 (RS) [P1, k1] 7 times, p1—15 sts.
ROWS 2 AND 4 (WS) [P1, k1] 3 times, p3, [k1, p1] 3 times—15 sts.
ROW 5 (RS) [P1, K1] 3 times, p1, insert LH needle into horizontal strand between last st worked and next st on needle and k1 tbl in loop (M1), k1, M1, [p1, k1] 3 times, p1—17 sts.
ROWS 6 AND 8 [P1, k1] 3 times, k3, [p1, k1] 3 times, p1.
ROW 7 P1, *k1, p1; rep from * to end.
ROW 9 [P1, k1] 4 times, insert LH needle into horizontal strand between last st worked and next st on needle and p1 tbl in loop (M1P), k1, M1P, [k1, p1] 4 times—19 sts.
ROWS 10 AND 12 [P1, k1] 4 times, p3, [k1, p1] 4 times.
ROW 11 P1, *k1, p1; rep from * to end.
Continue working this increase every 4th row as established.

the anatomy of seed stitch

DECREASE STITCH PATTERN

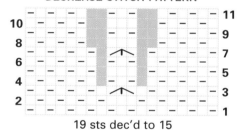

19 sts dec'd to 15

STITCH KEY

☐ k on RS, p on WS	▨ no stitch
⊟ p on RS, k on WS	◿▨◺ S2KP

DECREASING IN THE MIDDLE
OF A FLAT PIECE OF WORK
(beginning with 19 sts)
ROW 1 (RS) P1, *k1, p1; rep from * to end.
ROW 2 [P1, k1] 4 times, p3, [k1, p1] 4 times.
ROW 3 [P1, k1] 4 times, S2KP, [k1, p1] 4 times—17 sts.
ROW 4 P1, *k1, p1; rep from * to end.
ROW 5 [P1, k1] 3 times, p1, k3, [p1, k1] 3 times, p1.
ROW 6 P1, *k1, p1; rep from * to end.
ROW 7 [P1, k1] 3 times, p1, S2KP, [p1, k1] 3 times, p1—15 sts.
ROW 8 [P1, k1] 3 times, p3, [k1, p1] 3 times.
Continue working this decrease every 4th row as established.

If you're working a selvage stitch at each side of your work, increase as mentioned; only look at the third stitch on the needle instead of the second stitch.

DECREASING IN SEED STITCH
Like increases, decreases (reducing the number of stitches) shape a piece of knitting, and many types of decreases can be used in seed stitch. I prefer knitting or purling two stitches together. Once the first stitch has been decreased, by either a purl decrease or a knit decrease, continue in pattern to the last two stitches and knit two together (k2tog) or purl two together (p2tog), depending on the pattern.

When decreasing at the beginning of the row, look at the third stitch on the needle. If it needs to be a knit stitch, then purl the first two stitches together; if it should be a purl stitch, then knit these first two stitches together.

When decreasing at the end of the row, work to the last three stitches. If the last stitch is to be a knit, purl the two stitches together before it. If it is to be a purl, then knit the two stitches together before it.

BINDING OFF IN SEED STITCH
Many patterns will suggest that you bind off a piece of knitting "in pattern." In seed stitch, this means that as you bind off, you work each stitch as if it were a normal row, alternating knit and purl stitches as you slip them off the needle.

GAUGE
Gauge, or "tension" in British patterns, is important to consider with seed stitch, as with all patterns. It ensures that the finished piece will be the correct size and, with garments, the correct fit. Most patterns suggest a 4"/10cm square gauge sample swatch, which must be worked in the same yarn and pattern stitch to be used for the project in order to be accurate. To make the swatch, cast on the number of stitches suggested in the pattern. Using the suggested needle, work the number of rows called for in the pattern, then bind off. Measure the swatch: if it is larger than 4"/10cm, make a new swatch using a smaller needle size, and repeat this process until the swatch is the correct measurement. If it is too small, repeat the above process using a larger needle size. If you are planning to block the finished piece, block the swatch before you measure it—though seed stitch lies very flat and therefore does not often need blocking.

Once you have the correct size needle to achieve the gauge, make the full piece using that needle size. The size of the needle given in the pattern is only a suggested size and varies from knitter to knitter. ■

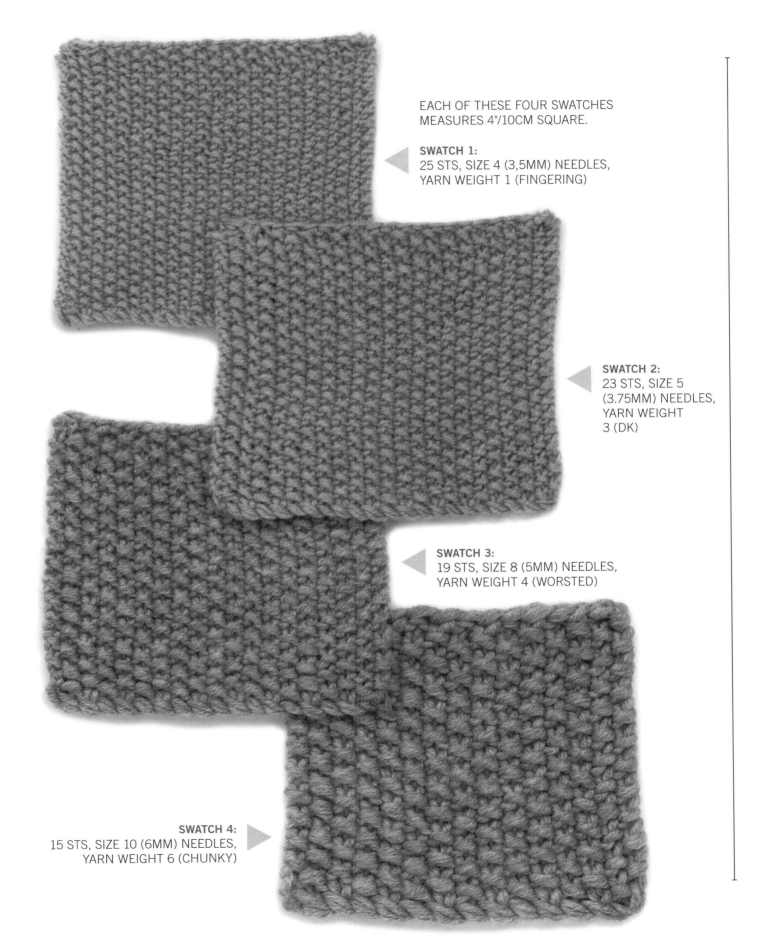

EACH OF THESE FOUR SWATCHES
MEASURES 4"/10CM SQUARE.

SWATCH 1:
25 STS, SIZE 4 (3,5MM) NEEDLES,
YARN WEIGHT 1 (FINGERING)

SWATCH 2:
23 STS, SIZE 5
(3.75MM) NEEDLES,
YARN WEIGHT
3 (DK)

SWATCH 3:
19 STS, SIZE 8 (5MM) NEEDLES,
YARN WEIGHT 4 (WORSTED)

SWATCH 4:
15 STS, SIZE 10 (6MM) NEEDLES,
YARN WEIGHT 6 (CHUNKY)

colorwork knitting

Many of the swatches and projects in this book use more than one color—usually two and sometimes three. However, only two colors are used in any one row, and with a little practice the technique is simple. The key is to avoid the two strands of yarn becoming entangled.

When one color is in use, the other color must be carried across the row on the wrong side until it is ready for use. There are two ways to carry the yarns across the back: either by "stranding" or by "weaving."

When working with two colors, you'll usually be following a chart showing the placement of each color. In seed stitch, the charts also indicate if the stitch is to be a knit stitch, represented by an empty square, or a purl stitch, represented by a "-" (see examples on page 47). Each square on the chart represents one stitch, and each row of squares represents one row of knitting. Charts are usually read from right to left when working the right side and odd-numbered rows, and left to right when working the wrong side and even-numbered rows. If the fabric is being worked in the round and the right side is always facing the knitter, each chart row is read from right to left. The charts often indicate the numbers of stitches in each pattern repeat, as well as any edge stitches not being repeated. If the patterns will be repeated over a given number of rows, this will also be indicated.

STRANDING
There are different ways to hold the yarns when knitting with two colors. Practice these methods in stockinette stitch and then in seed stitch until you are most comfortable with one method. Remember not to pull hard on the stranding yarns, as this will tighten and pucker the finished fabric. Carry the yarn not in use loosely across the back of the stitches.

DIFFERENT WAYS TO HOLD THE YARN
1. Holding one color in each hand: If you know how to knit both English-style (holding the working yarn A in your right hand) and Continental (holding the working yarn B in your left hand), this method is easy to master. On the right side, you will either knit or purl the next stitch with the color in your right hand. After a purl, return the right-hand yarn to the wrong side, then knit the next stitch with the color in your left hand. Repeat these two steps across the row or round.

2. Holding both colors in one hand (your left or right, depending on how you knit): Keep the yarns in the same position through the whole row or round, to prevent them from twisting. Pick up the color you need according to the chart and knit the next stitch. You can hold both the yarns over your index finger, or one over your index and the other over your middle finger. Some knitters hold both yarns against their palm, one strand over the index finger and the other held between the thumb and index finger. (These suggestions apply whether you're holding the yarn in your right or left hand.)

WEAVING
When is it preferable to use the weaving method? When one of the colors has to be carried over a large number of stitches (for example, five) on the wrong side, weaving helps prevent very long "floats."

When four or more stitches appear together on a chart in one color, you will need to twist the yarns around each other every few stitches. For example, if you need to work five stitches with color A, after working two or three stitches, place the color not being worked (in this case, color B) over the top of the working color A before knitting the next stitch, so that when you work the next color A stitch, the two yarns have been twisted.

In seed stitch, this method works best on a knit stitch. When working flat and on the wrong side of the work, the yarns will be at the front of the work and woven across the front in the same way. When working in rounds, the yarn is always carried at the back of the work, as the right side is always facing.

HOW TO AVOID A "JOG"
When working in the round with two colors, there can be a jog, or an interruption of the flow of the pattern, forming a kind of step. To avoid a jog, work the first round in pattern. When you come to the second round, slip the first stitch as if to purl, then work to the end of the round. Repeat these two rounds, carrying the color not in use up inside the first stitches of the new round. ■

ONE-HANDED ENGLISH STYLE

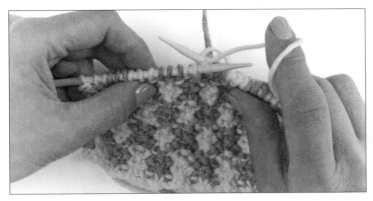

1. To knit color 1 on a right-side row, let the nonworking (gray) yarn drop to the back. Hold the working (ecru) yarn with your right index finger and bring it *over* the gray yarn to knit the next stitch.

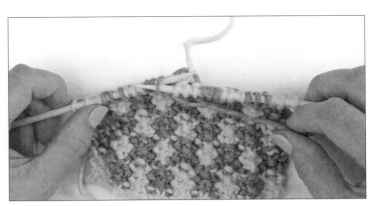

2. To purl color 2 on a right-side row, let the nonworking (ecru) yarn drop to the back. Bring the working (gray) yarn to the front *under* the ecru yarn and purl the next stitch.

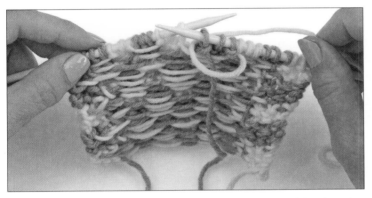

3. To knit color 1 on a wrong-side row, let the nonworking (gray) yarn drop to the front. Bring the working (ecru) yarn to the back between the needles and *over* the gray yarn to knit the next stitch.

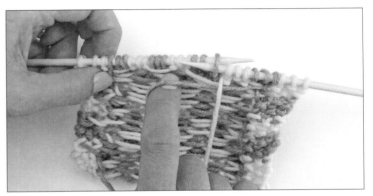

4. To purl color 2 on a wrong-side row, let the nonworking (ecru) yarn drop to the front. Bring the working (gray) yarn *under* the ecru yarn to purl the next stitch.

TWO-HANDED STRANDING

1. To knit color 1 on a right-side row, hold color 1 (ecru) with your right index finger and color 2 (gray) with your left index finger. Bring color 1 *over* color 2 and knit the next stitch.

2. To purl color 1 on a right-side row, keeping colors on right and left fingers as in step 1, and keeping color 2 at the back, bring color 1 *over* color 2 and to the front and purl the next stitch.

designing your own
seed stitch patterns & projects

Included in this book are two full-page grids (pages 140–141), one filled
with seed stitch and one with moss stitch, to use when designing patterns.

Note that if you start your pattern with a knit stitch when working
with more than one color, the effect will be different than if you
start with a purl stitch, as you can see with the swatches at right.

Make copies of the grids, and be creative charting your own
color patterns using colored pencils. You can also design
patterns on a stockinette stitch background, using the purl
stitches to make the designs (see examples).

If you want to vary a pattern—for example, using a child's hat
pattern to make an adult hat—you can change the weight of the
yarn, using a thicker yarn and the same number of stitches to
make the hat larger. The same process can be used for a wider
scarf or a more delicate scarf, using heavier or finer yarns.

When designing your own piece, work a swatch in the yarn you
are using for the project. I suggest a 6"/15cm swatch, as the larger
the swatch, the more accurate the gauge is. Measure the finished
swatch, then divide that measurement by the number of stitches
per inch. Do the same with the number of rows.

For example, if the swatch measures 6"/15cm and you cast
on 18 stitches and work 24 rows, divide 18 by 6—that gives you
the number of stitches per inch; in this case 3. Then divide the
number of rows, 24, by 6 to get a result of 4 rows per inch. To
make an 8-inch-wide scarf, you would cast on 24 sts, and you'd
produce 1 inch of length for every 6 rows worked.

When designing, you also have to determine how many stitches
are in the pattern repeat, For example, if the pattern repeat is a
multiple of 4 stitches plus 2, for an 8-inch scarf you would cast on
24 stitches plus 2: 26 sts.

Designing can be fun, so go ahead and be creative, and make
magic with those knit and purl stitches. I hope this book can be
a simple and effective tool and source of inspiration for you to try
different patterns using color and texture in seed stitch. ■

The seed stitch begins with a knit stitch.

The seed stitch begins with a purl stitch.

swatch gallery

SEED STITCH

(over an odd number of sts)

Cast on 25 sts.
ROW 1 (RS) K1, *p1, k1; rep from * to end.
ROW 2 (WS) K1, *p1, k1; rep from * to end.
Rep rows 1 and 2 for stitch pattern 30 times more—32 rows.
Bind off.
This pattern is reversible. ■

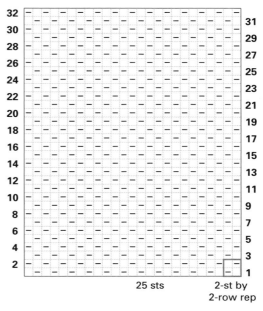

25 sts

2-st by
2-row rep

STITCH KEY

☐ k on RS, p on WS
⊟ p on RS, k on WS

MOSS STITCH

(over an odd number of sts)

Cast on 25 sts.
ROW 1 (RS) K1, *p1, k1; rep from * to end.
ROW 2 (WS) P1, *k1, p1; rep from * to end.
ROW 3 (RS) Rep row 2.
ROW 4 (WS) Rep row 1.
Rep rows 1–4 for stitch pattern 6 times more—28 rows.
Bind off.
This pattern is reversible. ■

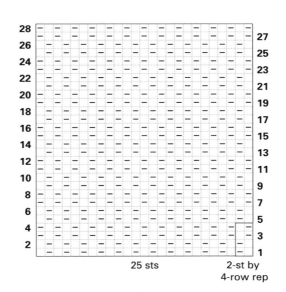

25 sts

2-st by
4-row rep

STITCH KEY

☐ k on RS, p on WS
⊟ p on RS, k on WS

DOUBLE MOSS STITCH

(multiple of 4 sts plus 2)

Cast on 22 sts.
ROW 1 (RS) K2, *p2, k2; rep from * to end.
ROW 2 (WS) P2, *k2, p2; rep from * to end.
ROW 3 P2, *k2, p2; rep from * to end.
ROW 4 K2, *p2, k2; rep from * to end.
Rep rows 1–4 for stitch pattern 6 times more.
Rep rows 1 and 2 once more—28 rows.
Bind off in pattern.
This pattern is reversible. ■

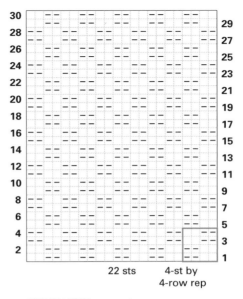

22 sts   4-st by
4-row rep

STITCH KEY

☐ k on RS, p on WS
⊟ p on RS, k on WS

CHEVRON SEED STITCH

(multiple of 20 sts plus 3)

Cast on 23 sts.
ROW 1 (RS) K1, *[p1, k1] twice, p1, k3, [p1, k1] twice, p1, k3, [p1, k1] twice; rep from * to last 2 sts, p1, k1.
ROW 2 (WS) K1, p1, * [k1, p1] twice, k1, p3, k1, p1, k1, p3, [k1, p1] 3 times; rep from * to last st, , k1.
ROW 3 K1, *k2, [p1, k1] twice, p1, k3, p1, k3, [p1, k1] twice, p1, k1; rep from * to last 2 sts, k2.
ROW 4 K1, p1, *p2, [k1, p1] twice, k1, p5, [k1, p1] twice, k1, p3; rep from * to last st, k1.
ROW 5 K1, *p1, k3, [p1, k1] twice, p1, k3, [p1, k1] twice, p1, k3; rep from * to last 2 sts p1, k1.
ROW 6 K1, p1, *k1, p3, [k1, p1] twice, k1, p1, [k1, p1] twice, k1, k3, k1, p1; rep from * to last st, k1.
ROW 7 K1, *p1, k1, p1, k3, [p1, k1] 4 times, p1, k3, p1, k1; rep from * to last 2 sts, p1, k1.
ROW 8 K1, p1, *k1, p1, k1, p3, [k1, p1] 3 times, k1, p3, [k1, p1] twice; rep from * to last st, k1.
Rep rows 1–8 for stitch pattern twice more—24 rows.
ROWS 25–27 Rep rows 1–3.
Bind off knitwise. ■

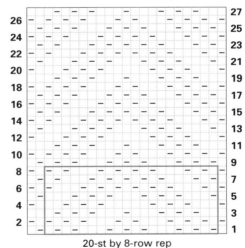

20-st by 8-row rep

23 sts

STITCH KEY

☐ k on RS, p on WS
⊟ p on RS, k on WS

DIAGONAL SEED STITCH

(multiple of 6 sts)

Cast on 24 sts.
ROW 1 (RS) *K3, p1, k1, p1; rep from * to end.
ROW 2 (WS) *P1, k1, p1, k1, p2; rep from * to end.
ROW 3 *K1, p1, k1, p1, k2; rep from * to end.
ROW 4 *P3, k1, p1, k1; rep from * to end.
ROW 5 *K1, p1, k3, p1; rep from * to end.
ROW 6 *P1, k1, p3, k1; rep from * to end.
Rep rows 1–6 for stitch pattern 4 times more—30 rows.
Bind off in pattern. ■

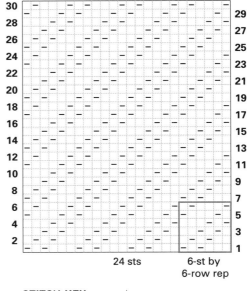

24 sts

6-st by
6-row rep

STITCH KEY

☐ k on RS, p on WS
⊟ p on RS, k on WS

ZIGZAG SEED STITCH

(multiple of 6 sts plus 2)

Cast on 26 sts.
ROW 1 (RS) *P1, k1, p1, k3, rep from * to last 2 sts, p1, k1.
ROW 2 (WS) K1, p1, *p2, [k1, p1] twice; rep from * to end.
ROW 3 *K2, [p1, k1] twice; rep from * to last 2 sts, k2.
ROW 4 P2, *k1, p1, k1, p3; rep from * to end.
ROW 5 *P1, k3, p1, k1; rep from * to last 2 sts, p1, k1.
ROW 6 K1, p1, *k1, p3, k1, p1; rep from * to end.
ROW 7 *P1, k3, p1, k1; rep from * to last 2 sts, p1, k1.
ROW 8 P2, *k1, p1, k1, p3; rep from * to end.
ROW 9 *K2, [p1, k1] twice; rep from * to last 2 sts, k2.
ROW 10 K1, p1, *p2, [k1, p1] twice; rep from * to end.
Rep rows 1–10 for stitch pattern twice more—30 rows.
Bind off purlwise. ■

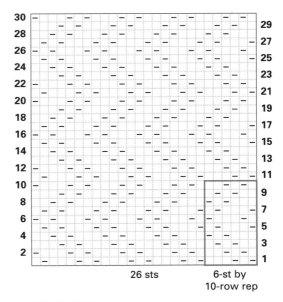

26 sts

6-st by
10-row rep

STITCH KEY

☐ k on RS, p on WS
⊟ p on RS, k on WS

23

CABLES ON SEED STITCH

STITCH GLOSSARY
4-ST LC Sl 2 sts to cn, hold to *front*, k2, k2 from cn.

(multiple of 7 sts plus 3)
Cast on 24 sts.
ROW 1 (RS) *P1, k1, p1, k4; rep from * to last 3 sts, p1, k1, p1.
ROW 2 (WS) P1, k1, p1, *p4, p1, k1, p1; rep from * to end.
ROW 3 *P1, k1, p1, 4-st LC; rep from * to last 3 sts, p1, k1, p1.
ROW 4 Rep row 2.
Rep rows 1–4 for stitch pattern 7 times more—32 rows.
Bind off in pattern. ∎

STITCH KEY

☐ k on RS, p on WS
⊟ p on RS, k on WS
▨ 4-st LC

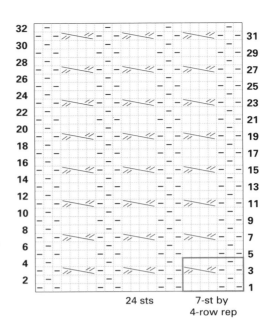

24 sts

7-st by
4-row rep

BROKEN CABLES

STITCH GLOSSARY
6-ST LPC1 Sl 3 st to cn and hold to *front*, k3, p1, k1, p1 from cn.
6-ST LPC2 Sl 3 st to cn and hold to *front*, p1, k1, p1, k3 from cn.

(multiple of 6 sts plus 4)
Cast on 28 sts.
ROW 1 (RS) K2, *p1, k1, p1, k3; rep from * to last 2 sts, k2.
ROW 2 (WS) K2, *p3, p1, k1, p1; rep from * to last 2 sts, k2.
ROWS 3 AND 4 Rep rows 1 and 2.
ROW 5 K2, *6-st LPC1; rep from * to last 2 sts, k2.
ROW 6 K2, *p1, k1, p1, p3; rep from * to last 2 sts, k2.
ROW 7 K2, *k3, p1, k1, p1; rep from * to last 2 sts, k2.
ROW 8 Rep row 6.
ROWS 9–12 Rep rows 7 and 8 twice.
ROW 13 K2, *6-st LPC2; rep from * to last 2 sts, k2.
ROW 14 Rep row 2.
ROW 15 Rep row 1.
ROWS 16–20 Rep rows 14 and 15 twice.
ROWS 21–36 Rep rows 5–20 for stitch pattern once.
ROWS 37–41 Rep rows 5–9.
Bind off in pattern. ∎

STITCH KEY

☐ k on RS, p on WS
⊟ p on RS, k on WS
▨ 6-st LPC1
▨ 6-st LPC2

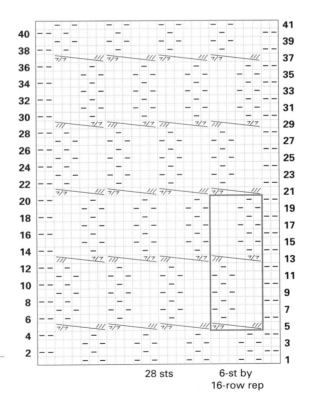

28 sts

6-st by
16-row rep

CHECKED SEEDED BASKET

(multiple of 6 sts plus 4)

Cast on 28 sts.
ROW 1 (RS) Knit.
ROW 2 (WS) Purl.
ROWS 3 AND 5 *K1, sl 2 wyib, p1, k1, p1; rep from * to last 4 sts, k1, sl 2 wyib, k1.
ROWS 4 AND 6 K1, sl 2 wyif, k1, *p1, k1, p1, sl 2 wyif, k1; rep from * to end.
ROW 7 Knit.
ROW 8 Purl.
ROWS 9 AND 11 *[P1, k1] twice, sl 2 wyib; rep from * to last 4 sts, [p1, k1] twice.
ROWS 10 AND 12 [K1, p1] twice, *sl 2 wyif, [k1, p1] twice; rep from * to end.
Rep rows 1–12 for stitch pattern twice more—36 rows.
Bind off purlwise. ∎

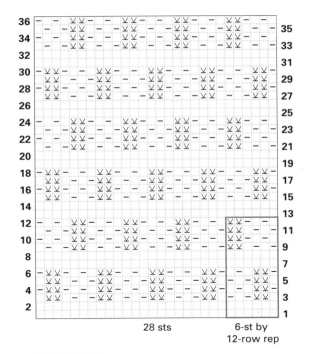

28 sts

6-st by
12-row rep

STITCH KEY

☐ k on RS, p on WS

⊟ p on RS, k on WS

⊻ slip 1 wyib on RS,
slip 1 wyif on WS

KING CHARLES BROCADE

(multiple of 12 sts plus 1)

Cast on 25 sts.
ROW 1 (RS) K1, *p1, k9, p1, k1; rep from * to end.
ROW 2 (WS) *K1, p1, k1, p7, k1, p1; rep from * to last st, k1.
ROW 3 K1, *p1, k1, p1, k5, [p1, k1] twice; rep from * to end.
ROW 4 *P2, k1, p1, k1, p3, [k1, p1] twice; rep from * to last st, p1.
ROW 5 K1, *k2, [p1, k1] 3 times, p1, k3; rep from * to end.
ROW 6 *P4, [k1, p1] twice, k1, p3; rep from * to last st, p1.
ROW 7 K1, *k4, p1, k1, p1, k5; rep from * to end.
ROW 8 Rep row 6.
ROW 9 Rep row 5.
ROW 10 Rep row 4.
ROW 11 Rep row 3.
ROW 12 Rep row 2.
Rep rows 1–12 for pattern.
Bind off. ∎

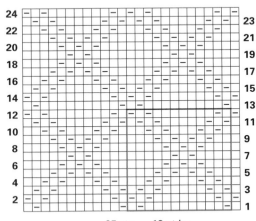

25 sts

12-st by
12-row rep

STITCH KEY

☐ k on RS, p on WS

⊟ p on RS, k on WS

INTERLOCKING TRIANGLES
(multiple of 10 sts plus 1)

Cast on 21 sts.
ROWS 1 AND 2 With A, k1, *p1, k1; rep from * to end.
ROW 3 *([K1, p1] twice)A, k1B, ([p1, k1] twice)A, p1B;
rep from * to last st, k1A.
ROW 4 K1A, *(p1, k1)B, (p1, k1, p1)A, (k1, p1)B, (k1, p1, k1)A;
rep from * to end.
ROW 5 *(K1, p1)A, (k1, p1, k1)B, (p1, k1)A, (p1, k1, p1)B;
rep from * to last st, k1A.
ROW 6 K1A, *([p1, k1] twice)B, p1A, ([k1, p1] twice)B, k1A;
rep from * to end.
ROW 7 *K1A, ([p1, k1] twice)B, p1A, ([k1, p1] twice)B;
rep from * to last st, k1A.
ROW 8 K1A, *(p1, k1, p1)B, (k1, p1)A, (k1, p1, k1)B,
(p1, k1)A; rep from * to end.
ROW 9 *(K1, p1, k1)A, (p1, k1)B, (p1, k1, p1)A, (k1, p1)B;
rep from * to last st, k1A.
ROW 10 K1A, *p1B, ([k1, p1] twice)A, k1B, ([p1, k1] twice)A;
rep from * to end.
ROW 11 *(K1, p1, k1)A, (p1, k1)B, (p1, k1, p1)A, (k1, p1)B;
rep from * to last st, k1A.
ROW 12 K1A, *(p1, k1, p1)B, (k1, p1)A, (p1, k1, p1)B,
(p1, k1)A; rep from * to end.
ROW 13 *K1A, ([p1, k1] twice)B, p1A, ([k1, p1] twice)B;
rep from * to last st, k1A.
ROW 14 K1A, *([p1, k1] twice)B, p1A, ([k1, p1] twice)B, k1A;
rep from * to end.
ROW 15 *(K1, p1)A, (k1, p1, k1)B, (p1, k1)A, (p1, k1, p1)B;
rep from * to last st, k1A.

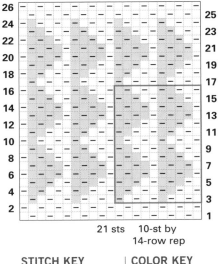

21 sts   10-st by
14-row rep

STITCH KEY
☐ k on RS, p on WS
⊟ p on RS, k on WS

COLOR KEY
☐ White (A)
▨ Light Blue (B)

ROW 16 K1A, *(p1, k1)B, (p1, k1, p1)A, (k1, p1)B,
(k1, p1, k1)A; rep from * to end.
Rows 3–16 form the stitch pattern.
ROWS 17–24 Rep rows 3–10.
ROWS 25 AND 26 Rep rows 1 and 2.
Bind off in pattern. ■

SPACED TRIANGLES
(multiple of 10 sts plus 1)

With A, cast on 21 sts.
ROWS 1 AND 2 With A, k1, *p1, k1; rep from * to end.
ROW 3 *([K1, p1] twice)A, k1B, ([p1, k1] twice)A, p1B; rep from *
to last st, k1A.
ROW 4 K1A, *(p1, k1)B, (p1, k1, p1)A, (k1, p1)B, (k1, p1, k1)A;
rep from * to end.
ROW 5 *(K1, p1)A, (k1, p1, k1)B, (p1, k1)A, (p1, k1, p1)B;
rep from * to last st, k1A.
ROW 6 K1A, *([p1, k1] twice)B, p1A, ([k1, p1] twice)B, k1A;
rep from * to end.
ROWS 7 AND 8 Rep rows 1 and 2.
Rep rows 1–8 for stitch pattern twice more—24 rows.
Bind off in pattern. ■

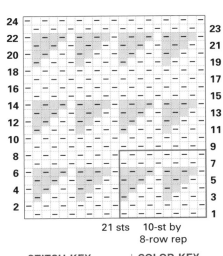

21 sts   10-st by
8-row rep

STITCH KEY
☐ k on RS, p on WS
⊟ p on RS, k on WS

COLOR KEY
☐ White (A)
▨ Light Blue (B)

STAGGERED WINDOWPANE

(over 25 sts)

With A, cast on 25 sts.
ROWS 1 AND 2 With A, k1, *p1, k1; rep from * to end.
ROWS 3 AND 4 With B, k1, *p1, k1; rep from * to end.
ROW 5–10 (K1, p1)A, *k1B, (p1, k1, p1)A; rep from * to last 3 sts, k1B, (p1, k1)A.
ROWS 11 AND 12 Rep rows 3 and 4.
ROWS 13–18 ([K1, p1] twice)A, *k1B, (p1, k1, p1)A; rep from * to last 5 sts, k1B, ([p1, k1] twice)A.
ROWS 19 AND 20 Rep rows 3 and 4.
ROWS 21–26 Rep rows 5–10.
ROWS 27 AND 28 Rep rows 3 and 4.
ROWS 29 AND 30 With A, k1, *p1, k1; rep from * to end.
Bind off in pattern. ■

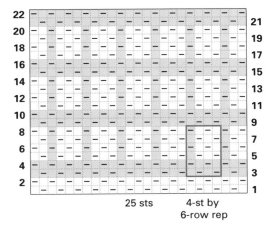

25 sts   4-st by
              16-row rep

STITCH KEY	COLOR KEY
☐ k on RS, p on WS	☐ k on RS, p on WS
⊟ p on RS, k on WS	⊟ p on RS, k on WS

WINDOWPANE GRID

(multiple of 4 sts plus 1)

With A, cast on 25 sts.
ROW 1 (RS) K1, *p1, k1; rep from * to end.
ROW 2 (WS) Rep row 1.
ROW 3 AND 4 With B, rep rows 1 and 2.
ROWS 5 AND 7 (K1, p1)A, k1B, *(p1, k1, p1)A, k1B; rep from * to last 2 sts, (p1, k1)A.
ROWS 6 AND 8 (K1, p1)A, *k1B, (p1, k1, p1)A; rep from * to last 3 sts, k1B, (p1, k1)A.
Rep rows 3–8 for stitch pattern twice more—20 rows.
ROWS 21 AND 22 Rep rows 3 and 4.
With A, bind off in pattern. ■

25 sts   4-st by
              6-row rep

STITCH KEY	COLOR KEY
☐ k on RS, p on WS	☐ White (A)
⊟ p on RS, k on WS	▨ Light Blue (B)

ZIGZAG STRIPES

(multiple of 4 sts plus 1)

With A, cast on 21 sts.
ROWS 1 AND 2 With A, p1, *k1, p1; rep from * to end.
ROW 3 P1A, *k1B, (p1, k1, p1)A; rep from * to end.
ROW 4 *P1B, k1A, (p1, k1)B; rep from * to last st, p1A.
ROW 5 P1A, *k1A, (p1, k1, p1)B; rep from * to end.
ROW 6 *P1A, k1B, (p1, k1)A; rep from * to last st, p1A.
Rep rows 1–6 for stitch pattern 4 times more—30 rows.
ROWS 31 AND 32 Rep rows 1 and 2.
Bind off in pattern. ■

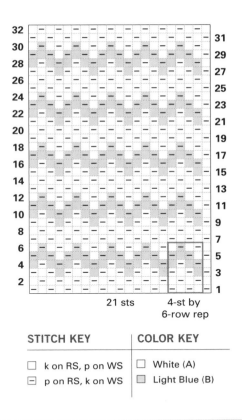

21 sts

4-st by
6-row rep

VERTICAL STRIPED MOSS STITCH

(multiple of 2 sts plus 1)

Cast on 25 sts using 2 colors as foll:
*1A, 1B; rep from * to last st, 1A.
ROW 1 (RS) K1A, *p1B, k1A; rep from * to end.
ROW 2 (WS) P1A, *k1B, p1A; rep from * to end.
ROW 3 P1A, *k1B, p1A; rep from * to end.
ROW 4 K1A, *p1B, k1A; rep from * to end.
Rep rows 1–4 for stitch pattern 5 times more—24 rows.
Bind off in pattern. ■

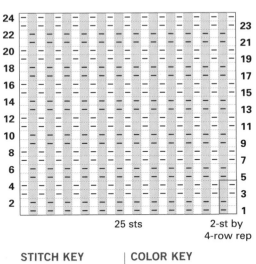

25 sts

2-st by
4-row rep

DIAMONDS & ZIGZAGS
(over 23 sts)

With A, cast on 23 sts.
ROWS 1 AND 2 With A, k1, *p1, k1; rep from * to end.
ROWS 3 AND 13 (RS) (K1, p1)A, (k1, p1, k1)B, (p1, k1, p1)A, (k1, p1, k1)B, p1A, (k1, p1, k1)B, (p1, k1, p1)A, (k1, p1, k1)B, (p1, k1)A.
ROWS 4 AND 12 (K1, p1)A, (k1, p1)B, (k1, p1, k1)A, (p1, k1, p1)B, (k1, p1, k1)A, (p1, k1, p1)B, (k1, p1, k1)A, (p1, k1)B, (p1, k1)A.
ROWS 5 AND 11 (K1, p1)A, k1B, (p1, k1, p1)A, (k1, p1, k1)B, ([p1, k1] twice, p1)A, (k1, p1, k1)B, (p1, k1, p1)A, k1B, (p1, k1)A.
ROW 6 AND 10 ([K1, p1] twice, k1)A, (p1, k1, p1)B, (k1, p1, k1)A, p1B, (k1, p1, k1)A, (p1, k1, p1)B, ([k1, p1] twice, k1)A.
ROWS 7 AND 9 ([K1, p1] twice)A, (k1, p1, k1)B, (p1, k1, p1)A, (k1, p1, k1)B, (p1, k1, p1)A, (k1, p1, k1)B, ([p1, k1] twice)A.
ROW 8 (K1, p1, k1)A, (p1, k1, p1)B, (k1, p1, k1)A, ([p1, k1] twice, p1)B, (k1, p1, k1)A, (p1, k1, p1)B, (k1, p1, k1)A.
ROWS 14–23 Rep rows 4–13.
ROW 24 Rep row 2. **ROW 25** Rep row 1. Bind off. ■

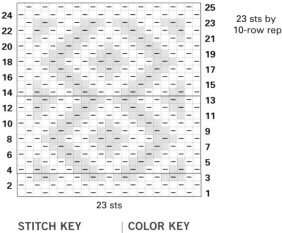

23 sts by
10-row rep

23 sts

STITCH KEY
☐ k on RS, p on WS
⊟ p on RS, k on WS

COLOR KEY
☐ White (A)
▨ Light Blue (B)

DIAMONDS, CROSSES, & DOTS
(multiple of 10 sts, plus 3)

With A, cast on 23 sts.
ROWS 1 AND 2 With A, k1, *p1, k1; rep from * to end.
ROW 3 K1A, *p1A, k1B, (p1, k1, p1)A, k1B, (p1, k1, p1)A, k1B; rep from * to last 2 sts, (p1, k1)A.
ROW 4 (K1, p1)A, *(k1, p1)B, ([k1, p1] twice, k1)A, (p1, k1)B, p1A; rep from * to last st, k1A.
ROW 5 K1A, *p1A, (k1, p1, k1)B, (p1, k1, p1)A, (k1, p1, k1)B; rep from * to last 2 sts, (p1, k1)A.
ROW 6 (K1, p1)A, *([k1, p1] twice)B, k1A, ([p1, k1] twice)B, p1A; rep from * to last st, k1A.
ROW 7 K1A, p1B, ([k1, p1] twice)A, *k1B, ([p1, k1] 4 times, p1)A; rep from * to last 7 sts, k1B, ([p1, k1] twice)A, p1B, k1A.
ROW 8 K1A, p1B, ([k1, p1] twice)A, k1B, *([p1, k1] 4 times, p1)A, k1B; rep from * to last 6 sts, ([p1, k1] twice)A, p1B, k1A.
Rows 1–8 form the lower border pattern.
ROW 9 K1A, *p1A, ([k1, p1] twice)B, k1A, ([p1, k1] twice)B; rep from * to last 2 sts, (p1, k1)A.
ROW 10 (K1, p1)A, *(k1, p1, k1)B, (p1, k1, p1)A, (k1, p1, k1)B, p1A; rep from * to last st, k1A.
ROW 11 K1A, *p1A, (k1, p1)B, ([k1, p1] twice, k1)A, (p1, k1)B; rep from * to last 2 sts, (p1, k1)A.
ROW 12 (K1, p1)A, *k1B, ([p1, k1] 3 times, p1)A, k1B, p1A; rep from * to last st, k1A.
ROW 13 K1A, *p1B, ([k1, p1] twice)A, k1B, ([p1, k1] twice)A, p1B; rep from * to last 2 sts, p1B, k1A.
ROW 14 K1A, p1B, *([k1, p1] twice)A, k1B, ([p1, k1] twice)A, p1B; rep from * to last st, k1A.
ROWS 15 K1A, *p1A, k1B, ([p1, k1] 3 times, p1)A, k1B; rep from * to last 2 sts, (p1, k1)A.
ROW 16 (K1, p1)A, *(k1, p1)B, ([k1, p1] twice, k1)A, (p1, k1)B, p1A; rep from * to last st, k1A.
ROW 17 K1A, *p1A, (k1, p1, k1)B, (p1, k1, p1)A, (k1, p1, k1)B; rep

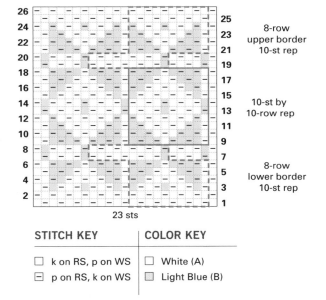

8-row
upper border
10-st rep

10-st by
10-row rep

8-row
lower border
10-st rep

23 sts

STITCH KEY
☐ k on RS, p on WS
⊟ p on RS, k on WS

COLOR KEY
☐ White (A)
▨ Light Blue (B)

from * to last 2 sts, (p1, k1)A.
ROW 18 (K1, p1)A, *([k1, p1] twice)B, k1A, ([p1, k1] twice)B, p1A; rep from * to last st, k1A. Rows 9–18 form the stitch pattern.
ROWS 19 AND 20 Rep rows 7 and 8.
ROW 21 K1A, *p1A, ([k1, p1] twice)B, k1A, ([p1, k1] twice)B; rep from * to last 2 sts, (p1, k1)A.
ROW 22 (K1, p1)A, *(k1, p1, k1)B, (p1, k1, p1)A, (k1, p1, k1)B, p1A; rep from * to last st, k1A.
ROW 23 K1A, *p1A, (k1, p1)B, ([k1, p1] twice, k1)A, (p1, k1)B; rep from * to last 2 sts, (p1, k1)A.
ROW 24 (K1, p1)A, *k1B, (p1, k1, p1)A, k1B, (p1, k1, p1)A, k1B, k1A; rep from * to last st, k1A.
ROWS 25 AND 26 Rep rows 1 and 2.
Rows 19–26 form the upper border pattern. Bind off in pattern. ■

35

EYELET STRIPES

(multiple of 2 sts plus 1)

With A, cast on 23 sts.
ROW 1 (RS) With A, k1, *p1, k1; rep from * to end.
ROW 2 (WS) With A, *p1, k1, p1; rep from * to last st, k1.
ROW 3 Rep row 1.
ROW 4 Rep row 2.
Attach B.
ROW 5 With B, k1, *yo, k2tog; rep from * to end.
ROW 6 With B, purl.
ROW 7 With B, k2, *yo, k2tog; rep from * to last st, k1.
ROW 8 With B, purl.
Rep rows 1–8 for stitch pattern twice more—24 rows.
ROWS 25–28 Rep rows 1–4.
With B, bind off purlwise. ■

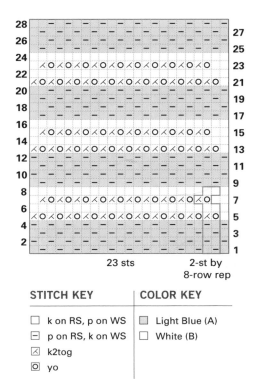

23 sts   2-st by
8-row rep

STITCH KEY	COLOR KEY
☐ k on RS, p on WS	▨ Light Blue (A)
⊟ p on RS, k on WS	☐ White (B)
◿ k2tog	
⊙ yo	

HONEYCOMB

NOTE
Carry A or B loosely up RH side of work when not in use.

(multiple of 8 sts plus 6)
With A, cast on 22 sts.
ROWS 1 AND 2 With A, knit.
ROWS 3 AND 5 With B, p1, k1, *sl 2 wyib, [k1, p1] 3 times;
rep from * to last 4 sts, sl 2 wyib, k1, p1.
ROWS 4 AND 6 With B, p1, k1, *sl 2 wyif, [p1, k1] 3 times;
rep from * to last 4 sts, sl 2 wyif, k1, p1.
ROWS 7–10 With A, knit.
ROWS 11 AND 13 With B, *[k1, p1] 3 times, sl 2 wyib;
rep from * to last 6 sts, [k1, p1] 3 times.
ROWS 12 AND 14 With B, *[p1, k1] 3 times, sl 2 wyif;
rep from * to last 6 sts, [p1, k1] 3 times.
ROWS 15 AND 16 With A, knit.
Rep rows 1–16 for stitch pattern once more—32 rows.
Bind off purlwise with A. ■

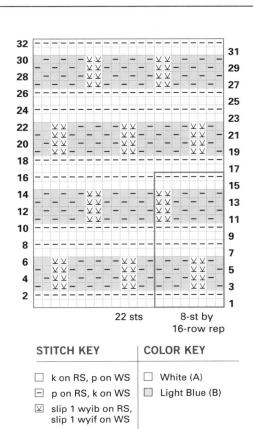

22 sts   8-st by
16-row rep

STITCH KEY	COLOR KEY
☐ k on RS, p on WS	☐ White (A)
⊟ p on RS, k on WS	▨ Light Blue (B)
⊻ slip 1 wyib on RS, slip 1 wyif on WS	

ONE-ROW STRIPES

STITCH GLOSSARY

SLIDE = Do *not* turn. Slide the sts back to the opposite end of needle to work next row from RS (WS).

NOTE

Use 2 double-pointed needles (dpn).

(over an odd number of sts)
With A, cast on 23 sts.
ROW 1 (RS) K1, *p1, k1; rep from * to end. Slide.
ROW 2 (RS) With B, p1, *k1, p1; rep from * to end. Turn.
ROW 3 (WS) With A, p1, *k1, p1; rep from * to end. Slide.
ROW 4 (WS) With B, k1, *p1, k1; rep from * to end. Turn.
ROW 5 (RS) With A, k1, *p1, k1; rep from * to end. Slide.
ROW 6 (RS) With B, p1, *k1, p1; rep from * to end. Turn.
Rep rows 3–6 for stitch pattern 7 times more—34 rows.
ROW 35 Rep row 3.
Bind off in pattern.
This pattern is reversible. ■

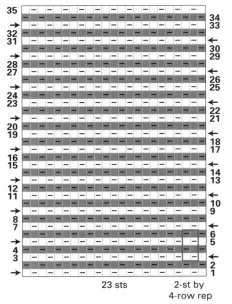

23 sts   2-st by 4-row rep

STITCH KEY

□ k on RS, p on WS
⊟ p on RS, k on WS
→ slide at end of row to work next row as RS
← slide at end of row to work next row as WS

COLOR KEY

□ White (A)
■ Dark Blue (B)

TWO-ROW STRIPED BEADED MOSS STITCH

STITCH GLOSSARY

SLIDE = Do *not* turn. Slide the sts back to the opposite end of needle to work next row from RS (WS).

NOTE

Use 2 double-pointed needles (dpn).

(over an odd number of sts)
With A, cast on 23 sts.
ROW 1 (RS) With A, k1, *p1, k1; rep from * to end. Turn.
ROW 2 (WS) With A, p1, *k1, p1; rep from * to end. Slide.
ROW 3 (WS) With B, k1, *p1, k1; rep from * to end. Turn.
ROW 4 (RS) With B, p1, *k1, p1; rep from * to end. Slide.
Rep rows 1–4 for stitch pattern 6 times more—28 rows.
Bind off in pattern.
This pattern is reversible. ■

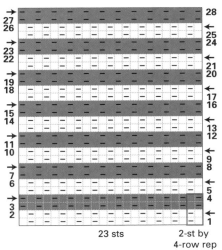

23 sts   2-st by 4-row rep

STITCH KEY

□ k on RS, p on WS
⊟ p on RS, k on WS
→ slide at end of row to work next row as RS
← slide at end of row to work next row as WS

COLOR KEY

□ White (A)
■ Dark Blue (B)

TWO-COLOR CHEVRON SEED STITCH
(multiple of 10 sts plus 3)

With A, cast on 23 sts.
ROW 1 (WS) K1A, p1B, *([k1, p1] twice)A, k1B, ([p1, k1] twice)A, p1B; rep from * to last st, k1A.
ROW 2 (RS) K1A, *(p1, k1)B, ([p1, k1] 3 times, p1)A, k1B; rep from * to last 2 sts, p1B, k1A.
ROW 3 K1A, p1B, *(k1, p1)B, ([k1, p1] twice, k1)A, (p1, k1, p1)B; rep from * to last st, k1A.
ROW 4 K1A, *([p1, k1] twice)B, (p1, k1, p1)A, (k1, p1, k1)B; rep from * to last 2 sts, p1A, k1B.
ROW 5 K1A, p1A, *([k1, p1] twice)B, k1A, ([p1, k1] twice)B, p1A; rep from * to last st, k1A.
ROW 6 K1A, *(p1, k1)A, ([p1, k1] 3 times, p1)B, k1A; rep from * to last 2 sts, p1A, k1A.
ROW 7 (K1, p1)A, *(k1, p1)A, ([k1, p1] twice, k1)B, (p1, k1, p1)A; rep from * to last st, k1A.
ROW 8 K1A, *([p1, k1] twice)A, (p1, k1, p1)B, (k1, p1, k1)A; rep from * to last 2 sts, p1, k1A.
ROWS 9–24 Rep rows 1–8 twice.
ROW 25 K1A, ([p1, k1] twice, p1)A, k1B, ([p1, k1] twice)A, p1B, ([k1, p1] twice)A, k1B, ([p1, k1]twice)A, p1B, k1A.
ROW 26 ([K1, p1] 11 times, k1)A.
Bind off in pattern. ■

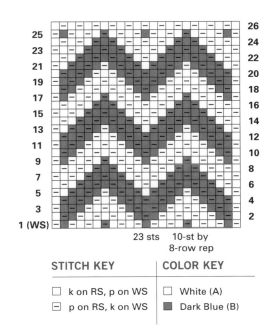

23 sts   10-st by 8-row rep

STITCH KEY
☐ k on RS, p on WS
⊟ p on RS, k on WS

COLOR KEY
☐ White (A)
■ Dark Blue (B)

TWO-COLOR CHEVRON SEED & STOCKINETTE
(multiple of 10 sts plus 3)

With A, cast on 23 sts.
SETUP ROW (WS) With A, purl.
ROW 1 (RS) K1A, *k1B, k4A, k1B, k4A; rep from * to last 2 sts, k1B, k1A.
ROW 2 P1A, k1B, *p1B, p7A, (p1, k1, p1)B; rep from * to last st, p1A.
ROW 3 K1A, *(k1, p1, k1)B, k5A, [k1, p1)B; rep from * to last 2 sts, k1B, p1A.
ROW 4 P1A, k1B, *(p1, k1, p1)B, p3A, ([p1, k1] twice)B; rep from * to last st, p1A.
ROW 5 K1A, *k1A, ([p1, k1] twice)B, k1A, ([k1, p1] twice)B; rep from * to last 2 sts, k2A.
ROW 6 P2A, *p1A, ([k1, p1] 3 times, k1)B, p2A; rep from * to last st, p1A.
ROW 7 K1A, *k3A, ([p1, k1] twice, p1)B, k2A; rep from * to last 2 sts, k2A.
ROW 8 P2A, *p3A, (k1, p1, k1)B, p4A; rep from * to last st, p1A.
ROW 9 K1A, *p1B, k4A, p1B, k4A; rep from * to last 2 sts, k1B, k1A.
ROWS 10–17 Rep rows 2–9.
ROWS 18–24 Rep rows 2–8.
ROW 25 K1A, *p1B, k4A; rep from * to last st, k1A.
ROW 26 With A, purl.
With A, bind off purlwise. ■

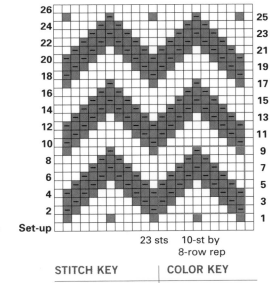

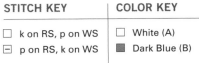

23 sts   10-st by 8-row rep

STITCH KEY
☐ k on RS, p on WS
⊟ p on RS, k on WS

COLOR KEY
☐ White (A)
■ Dark Blue (B)

BROKEN CHEVRON
(multiple of 20 sts plus 3)

With A, cast on 23 sts.
ROW 1 (RS) With A, K1, *p1, k1; rep from * to end.
ROW 2 (WS) K1A, p1B, *[k1A, p1B] twice, (k1, p1, k1)A, [p1B, k1A] 3 times, (p1, k1)A, [p1B, k1A] twice, P1B; rep from * to last st, k1A.
ROW 3 K1A, *[p1A, k1B] 3 times, (p1, k1, p1)A, k1B, p1A, k1B, (p1, k1, p1)A, [k1B, p1A] twice, k1B; rep from * to last 2 sts, (p1, k1A).
ROW 4 (K1, p1)A, *[k1A, p1B] 3 times, (k1, p1, k1)A, p1B, (k1, p1, k1)A, [p1B, k1A] 3 times, (k1, p1)A; rep from * to last st, k1A.
ROW 5 K1A, *(p1, k1, p1)A, [k1B, p1A] twice, k1B, ([p1, k1] twice, p1)A, [k1B, p1A] twice, k1B, (p1, k1)A; rep from * to last 2 sts, (p1, k1)A.
ROW 6 K1A, p1B, *(k1, p1, k1)A, [p1B, k1A] 3 times, (p1, k1)A, [p1B, k1A] 3 times, p1A, k1A, p1B; rep from * to last st, k1A.
ROW 7 K1A, *p1A, k1B, (p1, k1, p1)A, [k1B, p1A] 6 times, (k1, p1)A, k1B; rep from * to last 2 sts, (p1, k1)A.
ROW 8 K1A, p1B, *k1A, p1B, (k1, p1, k1)A, [p1B, k1A] 5 times, (p1, k1)A, p1B, k1A, p1B; rep from * to last st, k1A.
ROW 9 K1A, *[p1A, k1B] twice, (p1, k1, p1)A, [k1B, p1A] 4 times, (k1, p1)A, k1B; rep from * to last 2 sts, (p1, k1)A.
ROWS 10–25 Rep rows 2–9 for stitch pattern twice.
ROWS 26–28 Rep rows 2–4.
Bind off knitwise. ■

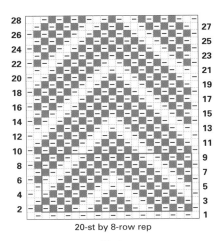

20-st by 8-row rep

23 sts

STITCH KEY	COLOR KEY
☐ k on RS, p on WS	☐ White (A)
⊟ p on RS, k on WS	■ Dark Blue (B)

DIAMONDS & DOTS
(multiple of 8 sts plus 1)

With B, cast on 25 sts.
ROW 1 (RS) *K1B, (p1, k1, p1)A, k1B, (p1, k1, p1)A; rep from * to last st, k1B.
ROW 2 (WS) K1A, *(p1, k1)A, p1B, k1A, p1B, (k1, p1, k1)A; rep from * to end.
ROW 3 *(K1, p1)A, k1B, (p1, k1, p1)A, k1B, p1A; rep from * to last st, k1A.
ROW 4 K1A, *p1B, ([k1, p1] twice, k1)A, p1B, k1A; rep from * to end.
ROW 5 *[K1B, (p1, k1, p1)A] twice; rep from * to last st, k1B.
ROW 6 K1A, *p1B, ([k1, p1] twice, k1)A, p1B, k1A; rep from * to end.
ROW 7 *(K1, p1)A, k1B, (p1, k1, p1)A, k1B, p1A; rep from * to last st, k1A.
ROW 8 K1A, *(p1, k1)A, p1B, k1A, p1B, (k1, p1, k1)A; rep from * to end.
Rep rows 1–8 for stitch pattern twice more—24 rows.
ROW 25 Rep row 1.
Bind off in pattern. ■

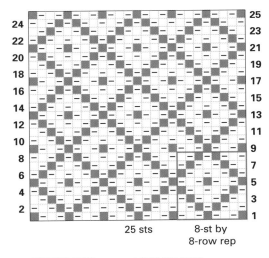

25 sts   8-st by 8-row rep

STITCH KEY	COLOR KEY
☐ k on RS, p on WS	☐ White (A)
⊟ p on RS, k on WS	■ Dark Blue (B)

BROKEN CROSSES STARTING WITH A KNIT

(multiple of 4 sts plus 3)

With A, cast on 23 sts.
ROW 1 (WS) (K1, p1, k1)A, *p1A, k1B, (p1, k1)A; rep from * to end.
ROW 2 *(K1, p1)A, k1B, p1A; rep from * to last 3 sts, (k1, p1, k1)A.
ROW 3 K1A, p1B, k1A, *(p1, k1, p1)B, k1A; rep from * to end.
ROW 4 *K1A, (p1, k1, p1)B; rep from * to last 3 sts, k1A, p1B, k1A.
ROW 5 (K1, p1, k1)A, *p1A, k1B, (p1, k1)A; rep from * to end.
ROW 6 *(K1, p1)A, k1B, p1A; rep from * to last 3 sts, (k1, p1, k1)A.
ROW 7 *(K1, p1)A, k1B, p1A; rep from * to last 3 sts, (k1, p1, k1)A.
ROW 8 (K1, p1, k1)A, *p1A, k1B, (p1, k1)A; rep from * to end.
ROW 9 *K1A, (p1, k1, p1)B; rep from * to last 3 sts, k1A, p1B, k1A.
ROW 10 K1A, p1B, k1A, *(p1, k1, p1)B, k1A; rep from * to end.
ROW 11 *(K1, p1)A, k1B, p1A; rep from * to last 3 sts, (k1, p1, k1)A.
ROW 12 (K1, p1, k1)A, *p1A, k1B, (p1, k1)A; rep from * to end.
ROWS 13–24 Rep rows 1–12 once.
With A, bind off in pattern. ■

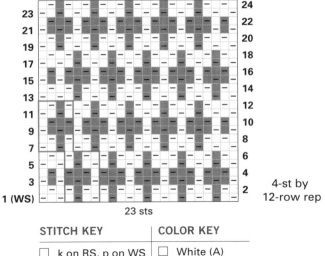

4-st by
12-row rep

23 sts

STITCH KEY

☐ k on RS, p on WS
⊟ p on RS, k on WS

COLOR KEY

☐ White (A)
■ Dark Blue (B)

BROKEN CROSSES STARTING WITH A PURL

(multiple of 4 sts plus 3)

With A, cast on 23 sts.
ROW 1 (WS) (P1, k1, p1)A, *k1A, p1B, (k1, p1)A; rep from * to end.
ROW 2 *(P1, k1)A, p1B, k1A; rep from * to last 3 sts, (p1, k1, p1)A.
ROW 3 P1A, k1B, p1A, *(k1, p1, k1)B, p1A; rep from * to end.
ROW 4 *P1A, (k1, p1, k1)B; rep from * to last 3 sts, p1A, k1B, p1A.
ROW 5 (P1, k1, p1)A, *k1A, p1B, (k1, p1)A; rep from * to end.
ROW 6 *(P1, k1)A, p1B, k1A; rep from * to last 3 sts, (p1, k1, p1)A.
ROW 7 *(P1, k1)A, p1B, k1A; rep from * to last 3 sts, (p1, k1, p1)A.
ROW 8 (P1, k1, p1)A, *k1A, p1B, (k1, p1)A; rep from * to end.
ROW 9 *P1A, (k1, p1, k1)B; rep from * to last 3 sts, p1A, k1B, p1A.
ROW 10 P1A, k1B, p1A, *(k1, p1, k1)B, p1A; rep from * to end.
ROW 11 *(P1, k1)A, p1B, k1A; rep from * to last 3 sts, (p1, k1, p1)A.
ROW 12 (P1, k1, p1)A, *k1A, p1B, (k1, p1)A; rep from * to end.
ROWS 13–24 Rep rows 1–12 once.
With A, bind off in pattern. ■

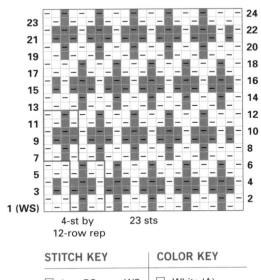

4-st by
12-row rep

23 sts

STITCH KEY

☐ k on RS, p on WS
⊟ p on RS, k on WS

COLOR KEY

☐ White (A)
■ Dark Blue (B)

INTERLOCKING DIAMONDS

(multiple of 6 sts plus 1)

With A, cast on 25 sts.
ROW 1 (WS) *(K1, p1, k1)A, p1B, (k1, p1)A; rep from *
to last st, k1A.
ROW 2 (RS) K1A, *(p1, k1)A, p1B, (k1, p1, k1)A; rep from * to end.
ROW 3 *(K1, p1)A, (k1, p1, k1)B, p1A; rep from * to last st, k1A.
ROW 4 K1A, *p1A, (k1, p1, k1)B, (p1, k1)A; rep from * to end.
ROW 5 *K1A, ([p1, k1] twice, p1)B; rep from * to last st, k1A.
ROW 6 K1A, *([p1, k1] twice, p1)B, k1A; rep from * to end.
ROW 7 *(K1, p1)A, (k1, p1, k1)B, p1A; rep from * to last st, k1A.
ROW 8 K1A, *p1A, (k1, p1, k1)B, (p1, k1)A; rep from * to end.
Rep rows 1–8 for stitch pattern twice more—24 rows.
ROW 25 *(K1, p1, k1)A, p1B, (k1, p1)A; rep from * to last st, k1A.
ROW 26 K1A, *(p1, k1)A, p1B, (k1, p1, k1)A; rep from * to end.
ROW 27 With A, *k1, p1; rep from * to last st, k1.
Bind off in pattern. ■

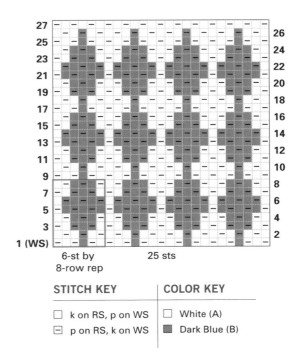

6-st by 8-row rep
25 sts

STITCH KEY

☐ k on RS, p on WS
⊟ p on RS, k on WS

COLOR KEY

☐ White (A)
■ Dark Blue (B)

TWEEDY CHECKS

(multiple of 4 sts plus 1)

With A, cast on 26 sts.
ROW 1 (RS) P1A, *k1A, p1B, (k1, p1)A; rep from * to last st, k1A.
ROW 2 (WS) K1A, *(p1, k1, p1)B, k1A; rep from * to last st, p1A.
ROW 3 P1A, *(k1, p1, k1)B, p1A; rep from * to last st, k1A.
ROW 4 K1A, *p1A, k1B, (p1, k1)A; rep from * to last st, p1A.
Rep rows 1–4 for stitch pattern 5 times more—24 rows.
ROW 25 With A, *p1, k1; rep from * to end.
Bind off in pattern. ■

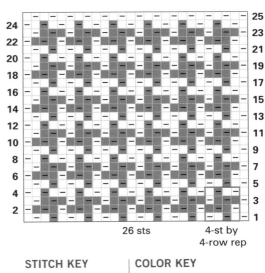

26 sts
4-st by 4-row rep

STITCH KEY

☐ k on RS, p on WS
⊟ p on RS, k on WS

COLOR KEY

☐ White (A)
■ Dark Blue (B)

PINSTRIPES
(multiple of 4 sts plus 3)

With A, cast on 23 sts.
ROW 1 (RS) K1A, *k1B, (k1, p1, k1)A; rep from * to last 2 sts, k1B, k1A.
ROW 2 (WS) K1A, p1B, *k3A, p1B; rep from * to last st, k1A.
Rep rows 1 and 2 for stitch pattern 15 times more—32 rows.
With A, bind off in pat. ■

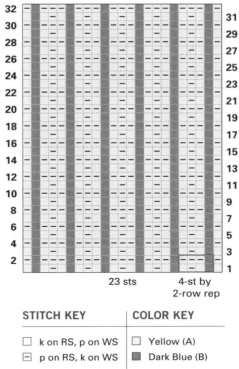

23 sts

4-st by
2-row rep

STITCH KEY

☐ k on RS, p on WS
⊟ p on RS, k on WS

COLOR KEY

☐ Yellow (A)
■ Dark Blue (B)

TWO-COLOR VERTICAL STRIPES
(multiple of 6 sts plus 3)

With B, cast on 27 sts.
ROW 1 (RS) *(P1, k1, p1)B, (k1, p1, k1)A; rep from * to last 3 sts, (p1, k1, p1)B.
ROW 2 (WS) Rep row 1.
Rep rows 1 and 2 for stitch pattern 12 times more—26 rows.
With B, bind off in pattern.
This pattern is reversible. ■

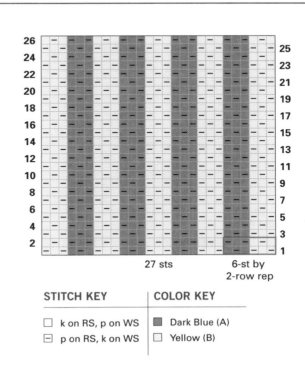

27 sts

6-st by
2-row rep

STITCH KEY

☐ k on RS, p on WS
⊟ p on RS, k on WS

COLOR KEY

■ Dark Blue (A)
☐ Yellow (B)

49

CHECKERBOARD PATTERN
(multiple of 6 sts plus 3)

With B, cast on 27 sts.
ROW 1 (RS) *(P1, k1, p1)B, (k1, p1, k1)A; rep from *
to last 3 sts, (p1, k1, p1)B.
ROW 2 (WS) (P1, k1, p1)B, *(k1, p1, k1)A, (p1, k1, p1)B;
rep from * to end.
ROW 3 Rep row 1.
ROW 4 Rep row 2.
ROW 5 With B, knit.
ROW 6 With B, purl.
ROW 7 *(P1, k1, p1)A, (k1, p1, k1)B; rep from * to last 3 sts,
(p1, k1, p1)A.
ROW 8 (P1, k1, p1)A, *(k1, p1, k1)B, (p1, k1, p1)A;
rep from * to end.
ROW 9 Rep row 7.
ROW 10 Rep row 8.
ROWS 11 AND 12 Rep rows 5 and 6.
Rep rows 1–12 for stitch pattern once more—24 rows.
With B, bind off. ■

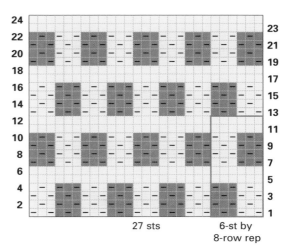

27 sts 6-st by 8-row rep

STITCH KEY	COLOR KEY
☐ k on RS, p on WS	■ Dark Blue (A)
⊟ p on RS, k on WS	☐ Yellow (B)

INTERLOCKING CHECKS
(multiple of 6 sts plus 3)

With B, cast on 27 sts.
ROW 1 (RS) *(P1, k1, p1)B, (k1, p1, k1)A; rep from *
to last 3 sts, (p1, k1, p1)B.
ROW 2 (WS) (P1, k1, p1)B, *(k1, p1, k1)A, (p1, k1, p1)B;
rep from * to end.
ROW 3 Rep row 1.
ROW 4 Rep row 2.
ROW 5 *(P1, k1, p1)A, (k1, p1, k1)B; rep from * to last 3 sts,
(p1, k1, p1)A.
ROW 6 (P1, k1, p1)A, *(k1, p1, k1)B, (p1, k1, p1)A;
rep from * to end.
ROW 7 Rep row 5.
ROW 8 Rep row 6.
Rep rows 1–8 for stitch pattern twice more—24 rows.
With B, bind off in pattern.
This pattern is reversible. ■

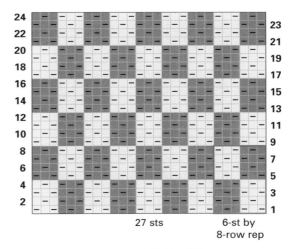

27 sts 6-st by 8-row rep

STITCH KEY	COLOR KEY
☐ k on RS, p on WS	■ Dark Blue (A)
⊟ p on RS, k on WS	☐ Yellow (B)

LARGE & SMALL CHECKS
(multiple of 8 sts plus 5)

With A, cast on 29 sts.
ROW 1 (RS) *([P1, k1] twice, p1)A, (k1, p1, k1)B; rep from *
to last 5 sts, ([p1, k1] twice, p1)A.
ROW 2 (WS) ([P1, k1] twice, p1)A, *(k1, p1, k1)B, ([p1, k1] twice,
p1)A; rep from * to end.
ROW 3 Rep row 1.
ROW 4 Rep row 2.
ROW 5 P1A, *(k1, p1, k1)B, ([p1, k1] twice, p1)A; rep from *
to last 4 sts, (k1, p1, k1)B, p1A.
ROW 6 P1A, (k1, p1, k1)B, *([p1, k1] twice, p1)A, (k1, p1, k1)B;
rep from * to last st, p1A.
ROW 7 Rep row 5.
ROW 8 Rep row 6.
Rep rows 1–8 for stitch pattern twice more—24 rows.
ROWS 25–28 Rep rows 1–4.
With A, bind off knitwise.
This pattern is reversible. ■

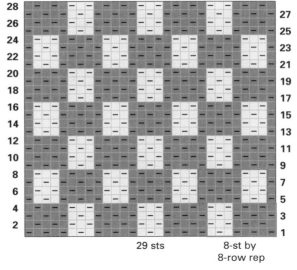

29 sts   8-st by 8-row rep

STITCH KEY	COLOR KEY
□ k on RS, p on WS	■ Dark Blue (A)
⊟ p on RS, k on WS	□ Yellow (B)

MINI DIAMONDS
(multiple of 8 sts plus 7)

With A, cast on 23 sts.
ROW 1 (WS) With A, *p1, k1; rep from * to last st, p1.
ROW 2 (RS) P1A, *(k1, p1)A, k1B, (p1, k1, p1)A, k1B, p1A;
rep from * to last 6 sts, (k1, p1)A, k1B, (p1, k1, p1)A.
ROW 3 (P1, k1)A, (p1, k1, p1)B, k1A, *([p1, k1] twice)A,
(p1, k1, p1)B, k1A; rep from * to last st, p1A.
ROW 4 P1A, *([k1, p1] twice, k1)B, (p1, k1, p1)A; rep from *
to last 6 sts, ([k1, p1] twice, k1)B, p1A.
ROW 5 (P1, k1)A, (p1, k1, p1)B, k1A, *([p1, k1]twice)A, (p1, k1, p1)
B, k1A; rep from * to last st, p1A.
ROW 6 P1A, *[(k1, p1)A, k1B, p1A] twice; rep from * to last 6 sts,
(k1, p1)A, k1B, (p1, k1, p1)A.
ROW 7 ([P1, k1] 3 times)A, *(p1, k1, p1)B, ([k1, p1] twice, k1)A;
rep from * to last st, p1A.
ROW 8 P1A, *k1B, (p1, k1, p1)A, ([k1, p1] twice)B; rep from *
to last 6 sts, k1B, (p1, k1, p1)A, k1B, p1A.
ROW 9 ([P1, k1] 3 times)A, *(p1, k1, p1)B, ([k1, p1] twice, k1)A;
rep from * to last st, p1A.
ROWS 10–25 Rep rows 2–9 for stitch pattern twice more.
ROW 26 Rep row 2.
ROW 27 Rep row 1.
With A, bind off in pattern. ■

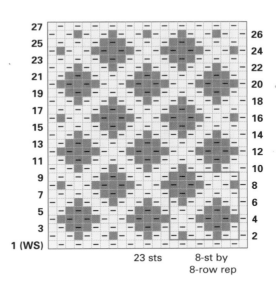

23 sts   8-st by 8-row rep

STITCH KEY	COLOR KEY
□ k on RS, p on WS	□ Yellow (A)
⊟ p on RS, k on WS	■ Dark Blue (B)

DIAMONDS ON STOCKINETTE
(multiple of 8 sts plus 7)

With A, cast on 23 sts.
ROW 1 (WS) With A, k1, p to last st, k1.
ROW 2 (RS) K1A, *k2A, k1B, k3A, k1B, k1A; rep from *
to last 6 sts, k2A, k1B, k3A.
ROW 3 (K1, p1)A, (p1, k1, p1)B, p1A, *p4A, (p1, k1, p1)B, p1A;
rep from * to last st, k1A.
ROW 4 K1A, *([k1, p1] twice, k1)B, k3A; rep from * to last 6 sts,
([k1, p1] twice, k1)B, k1A.
ROW 5 Rep row 3.
ROW 6 Rep row 2.
ROW 7 (K1, p5)A, *(p1, k1, p1)B, p5A; rep from * to last st, k1A.
ROW 8 K1A, *k1B, k3A, ([k1, p1] twice)B; rep from * to last 6 sts,
k1B, k3A, k1B, k1A.
ROW 9 Rep row 7.
ROWS 10–17 Rep rows 2–9 for stitch pattern once more.
ROWS 18–22 Rep rows 2–6.
ROW 23 Rep row 1.
ROW 24 With A, knit.
Bind off. ■

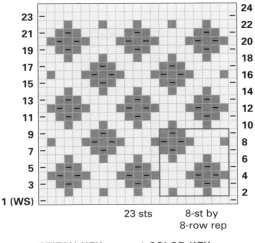

23 sts   8-st by
8-row rep

STITCH KEY	COLOR KEY
☐ k on RS, p on WS	☐ Yellow (A)
⊟ p on RS, k on WS	■ Dark Blue (B)

BROKEN DIAMONDS
(multiple of 8 sts plus 7)

With A, cast on 23 sts.
ROW 1 (WS) With A, k1, p to last st, k1.
ROW 2 (RS) K1A, *k2A, p1B, k3A, p1B, k1A; rep from *
to last 6 sts, k2A, p1B, k3A.
ROW 3 (K1, p1)A, (k1, p1, k1)B, p1A, *p4A, (k1, p1, k1)B, p1A;
rep from * to last st, k1A.
ROW 4 K1A, *([p1, k1] twice, p1)B, k3A; rep from * to last 6 sts,
([p1, k1] twice, p1)B, k1A.
ROW 5 Rep row 3.
ROW 6 Rep row 2.
ROW 7 (K1, p5)A, *(k1, p1, k1)B, p5A; rep from * to last st, k1A.
ROW 8 K1A, *p1B, k3A, ([p1, k1] twice)B; rep from * to last 6 sts,
p1B, k3A, p1B, k1A.
ROW 9 Rep row 7.
ROWS 10–17 Rep rows 2–9 for stitch pattern once more.
ROWS 18–22 Rep rows 2–6.
ROW 23 Rep row 1.
ROW 24 With A, knit.
Bind off. ■

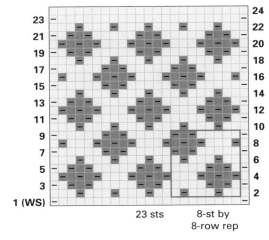

23 sts   8-st by
8-row rep

STITCH KEY	COLOR KEY
☐ k on RS, p on WS	☐ Yellow (A)
⊟ p on RS, k on WS	■ Dark Blue (B)

SEEDED & TWISTED CHECKS

STITCH GLOSSARY
3-ST LC Sl 1 st to cn and hold to *front*, k2, k1 from cn.

(multiple of 6 sts plus 3)
With A, cast on 27 sts. Knit 1 row on RS.
ROW 1 (WS) (K1, p1, k1)A, *p3B, (k1, p1, k1)A; rep from * to end.
ROW 2 (RS) *(K1, p1, k1)A, (3-st LC)B; rep from * to last 3 sts, (k1, p1, k1)A.
ROW 3 Rep row 1.
ROW 4 *(K1, p1, k1)A, k3B; rep from * to last 3 sts, (k1, p1, k1)A.
ROW 5 P3B, *(k1, p1, k1)A, p3B; rep from * to end.
ROW 6 *(3-st LC)B, (k1, p1, k1)A; rep from * to last 3 sts, (3-st LC)B.
ROW 7 Rep row 5.
ROW 8 *K3B, (k1, p1, k1)A; rep from * to last 3 sts, k3B.
ROWS 9–24 Rep rows 1–8 for stitch pattern twice more.
ROWS 25–28 Rep rows 1–4.
With A, bind off. ■

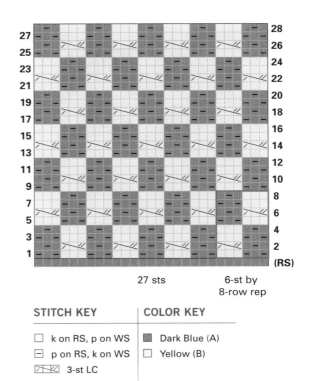

27 sts   6-st by 8-row rep

STITCH KEY	COLOR KEY
☐ k on RS, p on WS	■ Dark Blue (A)
⊟ p on RS, k on WS	☐ Yellow (B)
▨ 3-st LC	

SEEDED & TWISTED COLUMNS

STITCH GLOSSARY
3-ST LC Sl 1 st to cn and hold to *front*, k2, k1 from cn.

(multiple of 6 sts plus 3)
With A, cast on 27 sts. Knit 1 row on RS.
ROW 1 (WS) (K1, p1, k1)A, *p3B, (k1, p1, k1)A; rep from * to end.
ROW 2 (RS) *(K1, p1, k1)A, (3-st LC)B; rep from * to last 3 sts, (k1, p1, k1)A
ROW 3 Repeat row 1.
ROW 4 *(K1, p1, k1)A, k3B; rep from * to last 3 sts, (k1, p1, k1)A.
Rep rows 1–4 for stitch pattern 6 times more—28 rows.
With A, bind off. ■

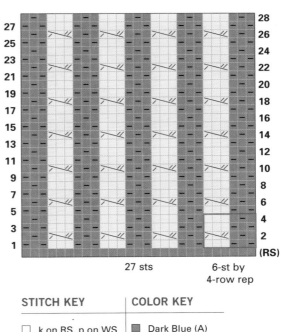

27 sts   6-st by 4-row rep

STITCH KEY	COLOR KEY
☐ k on RS, p on WS	■ Dark Blue (A)
⊟ p on RS, k on WS	☐ Yellow (B)
▨ 3-st LC	

TWO-ROW STRIPED SEED STITCH

(over an odd number of sts)

With A, cast on 25 sts.
ROW 1 (RS) With A, *k1, p1; rep from * to last st, k1.
ROW 2 (WS) With A, k1, *p1, k1; rep from * to end.
ROW 3 With B, *k1, p1; rep from * to last st, k1.
ROW 4 With B, k1, *p1, k1; rep from * to end.
Rep rows 1–4 for stitch pattern 7 times more—32 rows.
With B, bind off in pattern.
This pattern is reversible. ▨

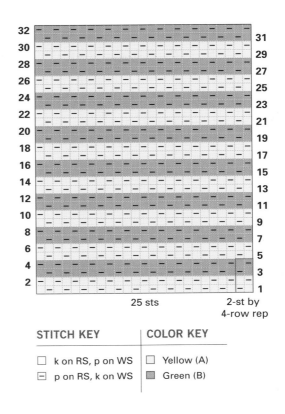

25 sts

2-st by
4-row rep

STITCH KEY	COLOR KEY
☐ k on RS, p on WS	☐ Yellow (A)
⊟ p on RS, k on WS	▩ Green (B)

TWO-ROW STRIPED MOSS STITCH

(over an odd number of sts)

With A, cast on 25 sts.
ROW 1 (RS) With A, *k1, p1; rep from * to last st, end k1.
ROW 2 (WS) With A, p1, *k1, p1; rep from * to end.
ROW 3 With B, *p1, k1; rep from * to last st, end p1.
ROW 4 With B, k1, *p1, k1; rep from * to end.
Rep rows 1–4 for stitch pattern 6 times more—28 rows.
Bind off in pattern.
This pattern is reversible. ▨

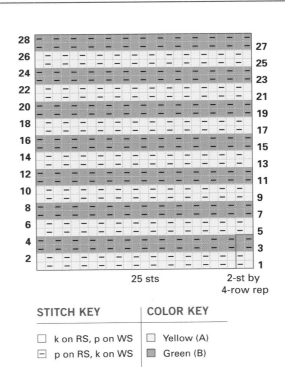

25 sts

2-st by
4-row rep

STITCH KEY	COLOR KEY
☐ k on RS, p on WS	☐ Yellow (A)
⊟ p on RS, k on WS	▩ Green (B)

VERTICAL STRIPED DOUBLE MOSS STITCH
(multiple of 4 sts plus 2)

Cast on 26 sts using 2 colors as follows: [2A, 2B] 5 times, 2A.
ROW 1 (RS) *K2A, p2B; rep from * to last 2 sts, k2A.
ROW 2 (WS) P2A, *k2B, p2A; rep from * to end.
ROW 3 *P2A, k2B; rep from * to last 2 sts, p2A.
ROW 4 K2A, *p2B, k2A; rep from * to end.
ROWS 5–20 Rep rows 1–4 for stitch pattern 4 times.
ROW 21 Rep row 1.
ROW 22 Rep row 2.
Bind off in pattern with A and B.
This pattern is reversible. ■

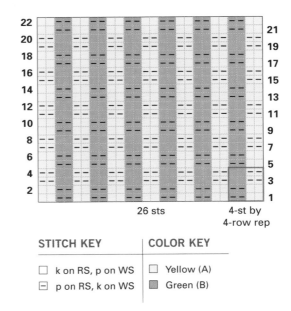

26 sts

4-st by 4-row rep

STITCH KEY

☐ k on RS, p on WS
⊟ p on RS, k on WS

COLOR KEY

☐ Yellow (A)
■ Green (B)

HORIZONTAL STRIPED DOUBLE MOSS STITCH
(multiple of 4 sts plus 2)

With A, cast on 26 sts.
ROW 1 (RS) With A, k2, *p2, k2; rep from * to end.
ROW 2 (WS) With A, p2, *k2, p2; rep from * to end.
ROW 3 With B, p2, *k2, p2; rep from * to end.
ROW 4 With B, k2, *p2, k2; rep from * to end.
ROWS 5–28 Rep rows 1–4 for stitch pattern 6 times.
ROW 29 Rep row 1.
ROW 30 Rep row 2.
With B, bind off in pattern.
This pattern is reversible. ■

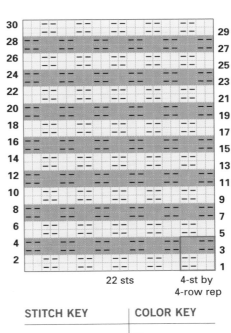

22 sts

4-st by 4-row rep

STITCH KEY

☐ k on RS, p on WS
⊟ p on RS, k on WS

COLOR KEY

☐ Yellow (A)
■ Green (B)

CHECKED DOUBLE MOSS STITCH
(multiple of 4 sts plus 2)

Cast on 26 sts using 2 colors as follows: [2A, 2B] 5 times, 2A.
ROW 1 (RS) *K2A, p2B; rep from * to last 2 sts, k2A.
ROW 2 (WS) P2A, *k2B, p2A; rep from * to end.
ROW 3 *P2B, k2A; rep from * to last 2 sts, p2B.
ROW 4 K2B, *p2A, k2B; rep from * to end.
Rep rows 1–4 for stitch pattern 5 times more—24 rows.
Bind off in pattern with A and B.
This pattern is reversible. ▪

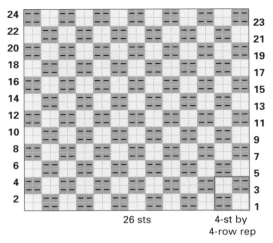

26 sts

4-st by
4-row rep

STITCH KEY

☐ k on RS, p on WS
⊟ p on RS, k on WS

COLOR KEY

☐ Yellow (A)
◼ Green (B)

SEED & STOCKINETTE STRIPES
(over an odd number of sts)

With A, cast on 23 sts.
ROW 1 (RS) With A, knit.
ROW 2 (WS) With A, purl.
ROWS 3 AND 5 With B, *k1, p1; rep from * to last st, k1.
ROWS 4 AND 6 With B, *k1, p1; rep from * to last st, k1.
ROWS 7 AND 24 Rep rows 1–6 for stitch pattern 3 times.
ROWS 25 AND 26 Rep rows 1 and 2.
With A, bind off knitwise.
This pattern is reversible. ▪

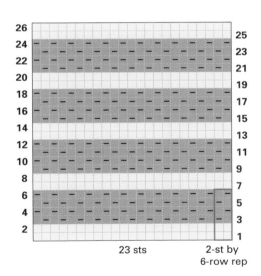

23 sts

2-st by
6-row rep

STITCH KEY

☐ k on RS, p on WS
⊟ p on RS, k on WS

COLOR KEY

☐ Yellow (A)
◼ Green (B)

DIAGONAL SEED & STOCKINETTE

(multiple of 6 sts)

With A, cast on 24 sts.
ROW 1 (RS) *K3A, (p1, k1, p1)B; rep from * to end.
ROW 2 (WS) *P1A, (k1, p1, k1)B, p2A; rep from * to end.
ROW 3 *K1A , (p1, k1, p1)B, k2A; rep from * to end.
ROW 4 *P3A, (k1, p1, k1)B; rep from * to end.
ROW 5 *(K1, p1)B, k3A, p1B; rep from * to end.
ROW 6 *(P1, k1)B, p3A, k1B; rep from * to end.
Rep rows 1–6 for stitch pattern 4 times more—30 rows.
With A, bind off knitwise. ■

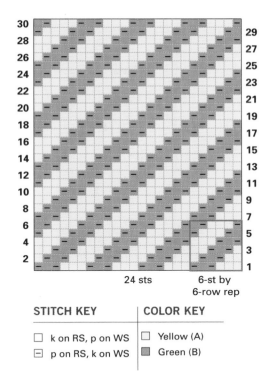

24 sts   6-st by
                6-row rep

STITCH KEY | **COLOR KEY**

□ k on RS, p on WS | □ Yellow (A)
⊟ p on RS, k on WS | ■ Green (B)

ZIGZAG SEED & STOCKINETTE

(multiple of 6 sts plus 2)

With A, cast on 26 sts.
ROW 1 (RS) *(P1, k1, p1)B, k3A, rep from * to last 2 sts, (p1, k1)B.
ROW 2 (WS) K1B, p1A, *p2A, (k1, p1, k1)B, p1A; rep from * to end.
ROW 3 *K2A, (p1, k1, p1)B, k1A; rep from * to last 2 sts, k2A.
ROW 4 P2A, *(k1, p1, k1)B, p3A; rep from * to end.
ROW 5 *P1B, k3A, (p1, k1)B; rep from * to last 2 sts, p1B, k1A.
ROW 6 (K1, p1)B, *(k1B, p3)A, (k1, p1)B; rep from * to end.
ROW 7 *P1B, k3A, (p1, k1)B; rep from * to last 2 sts, p1B, k1A.
ROW 8 P2A, *(k1, p1, k1)B, p3A; rep from * to end.
ROW 9 *K2A, (p1, k1, p1)B, k1A; rep from * to last 2 sts, k2A.
ROW 10 K1B, p1A, *p2A, (k1, p1, k1)B, p1A; rep from * to end.
ROWS 11–20 Rep rows 1–10 for stitch pattern once more.
ROWS 21–26 Rep rows 1–6.
With A, bind off purlwise. ■

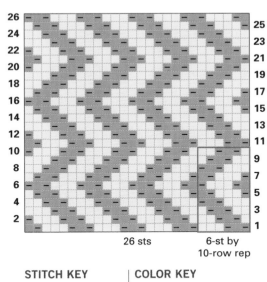

26 sts   6-st by
                10-row rep

STITCH KEY | **COLOR KEY**

□ k on RS, p on WS | □ Yellow (A)
⊟ p on RS, k on WS | ■ Green (B)

SLIP STITCH CHECKS

(multiple of 4 sts plus 1)

With A, cast on 25 sts.
ROW 1 (WS) With A, *k1, p1; rep from * to last st, k1.
ROWS 2 AND 4 (RS) K1B, *(p1, k1, p1)B, (sl 1 wyib)A; rep from *
to last 4 sts, ([p1, k1] twice)B.
ROWS 3 AND 5 ([K1, p1] twice)B, *(sl 1 wyif)A, (p1, k1, p1)B;
rep from * to last st, k1B.
ROWS 6 AND 8 (RS) With A, k1, *p1, k1; rep from * to end.
ROW 7 AND 9 (WS) With A, *k1, p1; rep from * to last st, k1.
ROWS 10–25 Rep rows 2–9 for stitch pattern twice more.
ROWS 26–30 Rep rows 2–6.
With A, bind off in pattern. ■

STITCH KEY	COLOR KEY
☐ k on RS, p on WS	☐ Yellow (A)
⊟ p on RS, k on WS	▣ Green (B)
☑ slip 1 wyib on RS, slip 1 wyif on WS	

STAGGERED SLIP STITCH CHECKS

(multiple of 6 sts plus 4)

With A, cast on 28 sts.
ROW 1 (RS) With A, knit.
ROW 2 (WS) With A, purl.
ROWS 3 AND 5 *K1B, sl 2 wyib, (p1, k1, p1)B; rep from *
to last 4 sts, k1B, sl 2 wyib, k1B.
ROWS 4 AND 6 K1B, sl 2 wyif, k1B, *(p1, k1, p1)B, sl 2 wyif, k1B;
rep from * to end.
ROW 7 Rep row 1.
ROW 8 Rep row 2.
ROWS 9 AND 11 *([P1, k1] twice)B, sl 2 wyib; rep from *
to last 4 sts, ([p1, k1] twice)B.
ROWS 10 AND 12 ([K1, p1] twice)B, *sl 2 wyif, ([k1, p1] twice)B;
rep from * to end.
Rep rows 1–12 for stitch pattern twice more, then rows 1 and 2 once.
With A, bind off purlwise. ■

STITCH KEY	COLOR KEY
☐ k on RS, p on WS	☐ Yellow (A)
⊟ p on RS, k on WS	▣ Green (B)
☑ slip 1 wyib on RS, slip 1 wyif on WS	

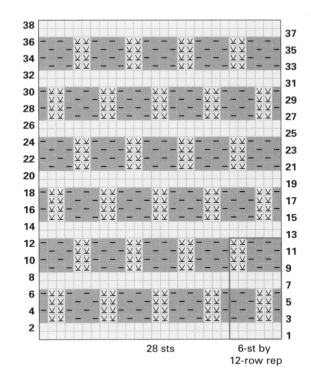

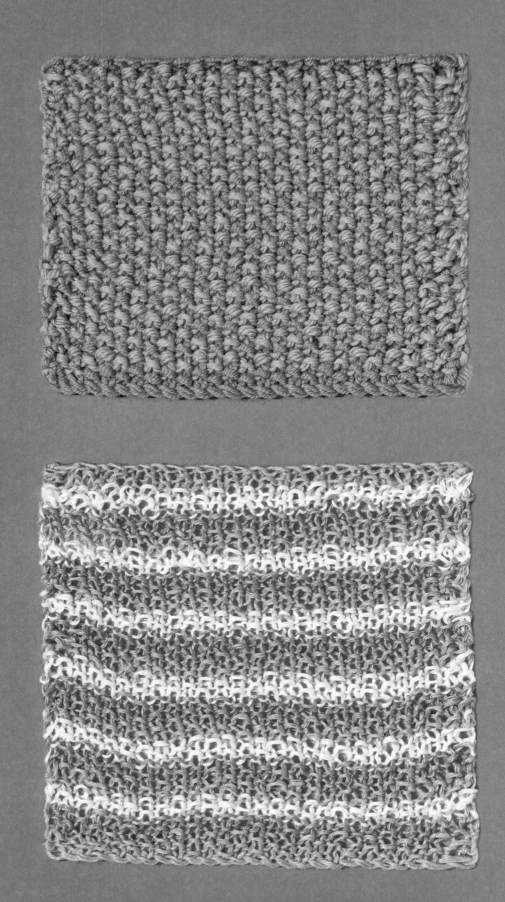

THREE-COLOR SEED STITCH

NOTE
Carry yarns not in use loosely up WS of work. The color needed to start each row will be at the correct side when needed.

(over an odd number of sts)
With A, cast on 27 sts.
ROW 1 (RS) With A, *p1, k1; rep from * to last st, end p1.
ROW 2 (WS) With B, p1, *k1, p1; rep from * to end.
ROW 3 With C, *p1, k1; rep from * to last st, end p1.
ROW 4 With A, p1, *k1, p1; rep from * to end.
ROW 5 With B, *p1, k1; rep from * to last st, end p1.
ROW 6 With C, p1, *k1, p1; rep from * to end.
ROWS 7–26 Rep rows 1–6 for stitch pattern 5 times more.
ROWS 37–40 Rep rows 1–4 once.
With A, bind off in pattern. ■

STITCH KEY	COLOR KEY
☐ k on RS, p on WS	■ Blue (A)
⊟ p on RS, k on WS	■ Turquoise (B)
	☐ Lilac (C)

2-st by
2-row rep

27 sts

THREE-COLOR 3-ROW SEED STITCH STRIPES
(over an odd number of sts)

With A, cast on 27 sts.
ROW 1 (RS) With A, *p1, k1; rep from * to last st, end p1.
ROW 2 With A, p1, *k1, p1; rep from * to end.
ROW 3 With A, *p1, k1; rep from * to last st, end p1.
ROW 4 With B, p1, *k1, p1; rep from * to end.
ROW 5 With B, *p1, k1; rep from * to last st, end p1.
ROW 6 With B, p1, *k1, p1; rep from * to end.
ROW 7 With C, *p1, k1; rep from * to last st, end p1.
ROW 8 With C, p1, *k1, p1; rep from * to end.
ROW 9 With C, *p1, k1; rep from * to last st, end p1.
ROWS 10–54 Rep rows 1–9 for stitch pattern 5 times.
ROWS 55–57 Rep rows 1–3 once.
With A, bind off in pattern.
This pattern is reversible. ■

STITCH KEY	COLOR KEY
☐ k on RS, p on WS	■ Turquoise (A)
⊟ p on RS, k on WS	☐ Lilac (B)
	☐ White (C)

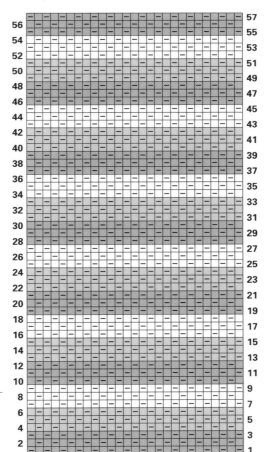

2-st by
9-row rep

27 sts

EYELET CHEVRON SEED STITCH

(multiple of 16 sts plus 1)

Cast on 33 sts.
ROW 1 (RS) K1, *yo, ssk, [p1, k1] 5 times, p1, k2tog, yo, k1; rep from * to end.
ROW 2 (WS) *K1, p1, yo, p2tog, [k1, p1] 4 times, k1, p2tog tbl, yo, p1; rep from * to last st, k1.
ROW 3 K1, *p1, k1, yo, ssk, [p1, k1] 3 times, p1, k2tog, yo, k1, p1, k1; rep from * to end.
ROW 4 *[K1, p1] twice, yo, p2tog, [k1, p1] twice, k1, p2tog tbl, yo, p1, k1, p1; rep from * to last st, k1.
ROW 5 K1, *[p1, k1] twice, *yo, ssk, p1, k1, p1, k2tog, yo, [k1, p1] twice, k1; rep from * to end.
ROW 6 *[K1, p1] 3 times, yo, p2tog, k1, p2tog tbl, yo,

[p1, k1] twice, p1; rep from * to last st, k1.
ROW 7 K1, *[p1, k1] 3 times, yo, S2KP, yo, [k1, p1] 3 times, k1; rep from * to end.
ROWS 8 AND 10 *K1, p1; rep from * to last st, k1.
ROWS 9 AND 11 K1, *p1, k1; rep from * to end.
ROW 12 *K1, p1; rep from * to last st, k1. Rep rows 1–12 for lace chevron with seed stitch pattern twice more—36 rows. Bind off. ■

STITCH KEY

☐ k on RS, p on WS
⊟ p on RS, k on WS
☒ k2tog on RS, p2tog on WS
⊠ ssk on RS, p2tog tbl on WS
⊼ S2KP
Ⓞ yo

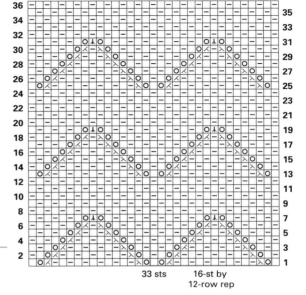

33 sts   16-st by 12-row rep

DIAGONAL SEED & STOCKINETTE STRIPES

STITCH GLOSSARY
K-P Knit and then purl into same st.
P-K Purl and then knit into same st.

(over an odd number of sts)
Cast on 3 sts.
ROW 1 (RS) K1, p1, k1.
ROW 2 (WS) K1, p1, k1.
ROW 3 (INC) P-K, p1, K-P.
ROW 4 [P1, k1] twice, p1.
ROW 5 (INC) K-P, k1, p1, k1, P-K.
ROW 6 [K1, p1] 3 times, k1.
ROW 7 (INC) P-K, *p1, k1; rep from * to last 2 sts, p1, K-P.
ROW 8 *P1, k1; rep from * to last st, p1.
ROW 9 (INC) K-P, *k1, p1; rep from * to last 2 sts, k1, P-K.
ROW 10 *K1, p1; rep from * to last st, k1.
NOTE: Rows [7–10] twice form the seed st section.
ROWS 11 AND 13 K-P, k to last st, K-P.
ROW 12 AND 14 Purl.
NOTE: Rows 11–14 form the St st section.
Cont as established, inc'ing 1 st each side every RS row, alternating 8 rows seed st and 4 rows St st.
NOTE: If the 2nd st on the needle in the seed st pat is a knit, then inc as P-K. If the 2nd st on the needle is a purl, then inc as K-P.
When 37 sts are on the needle, end RS row.
NEXT ROW (WS) P37.
Cont in pat as established. Dec 1 st each side every RS row, working k2tog or p2tog, depending on the pattern, until 3 sts rem.
Work 1 WS row.
Bind off 3 sts. ■

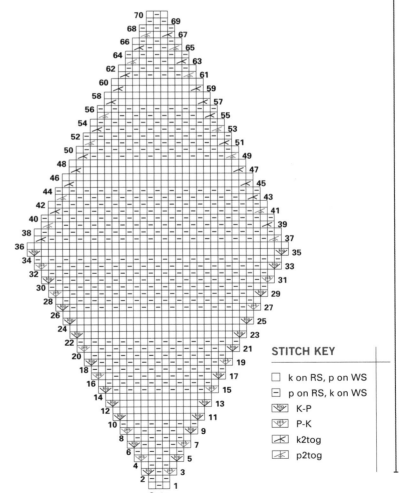

3 sts

STITCH KEY

☐ k on RS, p on WS
⊟ p on RS, k on WS
K-P
P-K
k2tog
p2tog

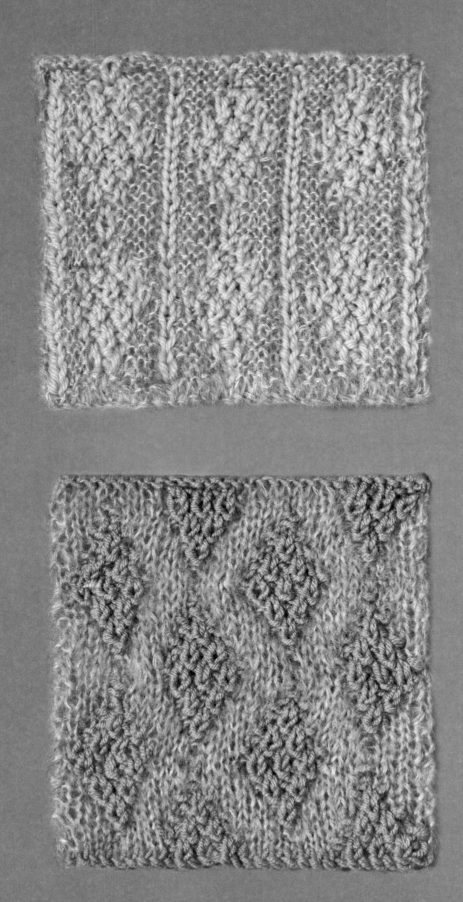

MOSS STITCH DIAMONDS ON REVERSE STOCKINETTE
(multiple of 10 sts plus 3)

With A, cast on 33 sts.
ROW 1 (RS) Purl.
ROW 2 P1, k to last st, p1.
Attach B.
ROW 3 P1A, *k1B, p4A, k1B, p4A; rep from * to last 2 sts, k1B, p1A.
ROW 4 AND ALL WS ROWS Keeping the first and last st as purl, work all other sts as they appear.
ROW 5 P1A, *k1B, p3A, k1B, p1B, k1B, p3A; rep from * to last 2 sts, k1B, p1A.
ROW 7 P1A, *k1B, p2A, [k1B, p1B] twice, k1B, p2A; rep from * to last 2 sts, k1B, p1A.
ROW 9 P1A, *k1B, p1A, [k1B, p1B] 3 times, k1B, p1A; rep from * to last 2 sts, k1B, p1A.
ROW 11 Rep row 7.
ROW 13 Rep row 5.
ROW 15 Rep row 3.
ROW 17 P1A, *k1B, p9A; rep from * to last 2 sts, k1B, p1A.
ROW 18 Rep row 4.
ROWS 19–32 Rep rows 3–16 once.
ROW 33 (RS) Rep row 1.
Bind off in pat. ∎

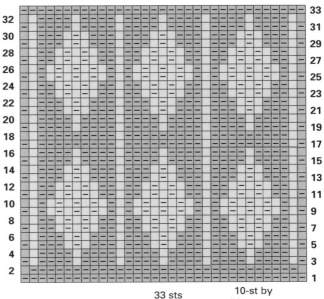

33 sts

10-st by 14-row rep

STITCH KEY	COLOR KEY
☐ k on RS, p on WS	▨ Blue Mohair (A)
⊟ p on RS, k on WS	☐ Mint Merino (B)

MOSS STITCH DIAMONDS ON STOCKINETTE
(multiple of 14 sts plus 2)

With A, cast on 30 sts.
Attach B.
ROW 1 (RS) K1B, *([p1, k1] 3 times)A, p1A, k7B; rep from * to last st, k1B.
ROW 2 AND ALL WS ROWS K1B, *k the knits and p the purls in colors as established; rep from * to last st, k1B.
ROW 3 K1B, *k1B, ([p1, k1] twice)A, p1A, k4B, p1A, k3B; rep from * to last st, k1B.
ROW 5 K1B, *k2B, (p1, k1, p1)A, k4B, (p1, k1, p1)A, k2B; rep from * to last st, k1B.
ROW 7 K1B, *k3B, p1A, k4B, ([p1, k1]twice)A, p1A, k1B; rep from * to last st, k1B.
ROW 9 K1B, *k7B, ([p1, k1] 3 times)A, p1A; rep from * to last st, k1B.
ROW 11 Rep row 7.
ROW 13 Rep row 5.
ROW 15 Rep row 3.
ROW 16 Rep row 2.
ROWS 17–32 Rep row 1–16 for pattern once.
ROW 33 Rep row 1.
Bind off on WS purlwise. ∎

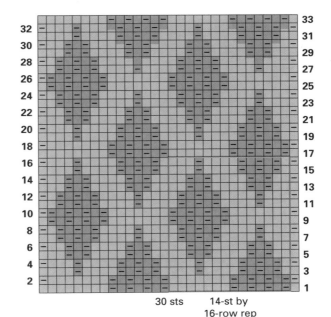

30 sts

14-st by 16-row rep

STITCH KEY	COLOR KEY
☐ k on RS, p on WS	▨ Blue Merino Yarn (A)
⊟ p on RS, k on WS	▨ Blue Mohair Yarn (B)

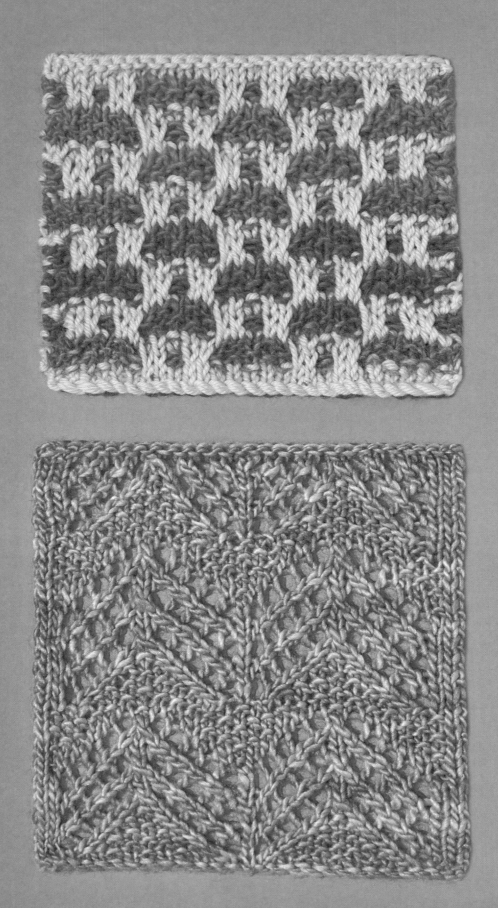

DOTS & DASHES
(multiple of 10 sts plus 7 plus 2 selvage sts)

With A, cast on 29 sts.
ROW 1 (RS) With A, knit.
ROW 2 (WS) With A, k1, p to last st, k1.
Attach B.
ROW 3 With B, k2, *[p1, k1] twice, p1,
sl 2 wyib, p1, sl 2 wyib; rep from * to
last 7 sts, [p1, k1] 3 times, k1.
ROW 4 With B, k1, [k1, p1] 3 times,
*sl 2 wyif, k1, sl 2 wyif, [p1, k1] twice,
p1; rep from * to last 2 sts, k2.
ROWS 5 AND 6 Rep rows 1 and 2.

ROW 7 With B, k1, p1, *sl 2 wyib, p1,
sl 2 wyib, [p1, k1] twice; rep from * to
last 8 sts, [p1, sl 2 wyib] twice, p1, k1.
ROW 8 With B, k1, [k1, sl 2 wyif] twice,
p1, *[k1, p1] twice, sl 2 wyif, k1,
sl 2 wyif, p1; rep from * to last st, k1.
ROWS 9–24 Rep rows 1–8 for stitch
pattern twice.
ROWS 25–30 Rep rows 1–6 once.
Bind off. ■

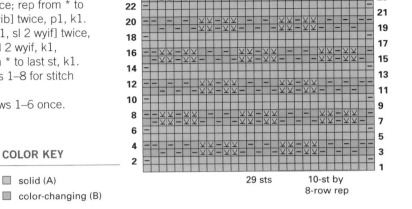

29 sts   10-st by
          8-row rep

STITCH KEY
☐ k on RS, p on WS
⊟ p on RS, k on WS
☑ slip 1 wyib on RS, slip 1 wyif on WS

COLOR KEY
▨ solid (A)
▧ color-changing (B)

LACE CHEVRON & SEED STITCH
(multiple of 12 sts plus 5)

Cast on 29 sts.
ROW 1 (WS) Purl.
ROW 2 (RS) K2, *k1, yo, ssk, [k1, p1] 3 times, k1,
k2tog, yo; rep from * to last 3 sts; k3.
ROW 3 P3, *p2, [k1, p1] 4 times, p2; rep from * to last
2 sts, p2.
ROW 4 K2, *k2, yo, ssk, [p1, k1] twice, p1, k2tog, yo, k1;
rep from * to last 3 sts, k3.
ROW 5 P3, *p4, k1, p1, k1, p5; rep from * to last
2 sts, p2.
ROW 6 K2, *k1, [yo, ssk] twice, k1, p1, k1, [k2tog, yo]
twice; rep from * to last 3 sts, k3.
ROW 7 Rep row 5.
ROW 8 K2, *k2, [yo, ssk] twice, p1, [k2tog, yo] twice, k1;
rep from * to last 3 sts, k3.
ROW 9 Purl.
ROW 10 K2, *k1, [yo, ssk] twice, yo, S2KP, yo, [k2tog, yo]
twice; rep from * to last 3 sts, k3.
ROW 11 Purl.
ROW 12 K2, *p1, k1, [yo, ssk] twice, k1, [k2tog, yo]
twice, k1; rep from * to last 3 sts, p1, k2.
ROW 13 Purl.
ROW 14 K2, *p1, k2, yo, ssk, yo, S2KP, yo, k2tog, yo, k2;
rep from * to last 3 sts, p1, k2.
ROW 15 P3, *k1, p9, k1, p1; rep from * to last 2 sts, p2.
ROW 16 K2, *[p1, k1] twice, yo, ssk, k1, k2tog, yo, k1, p1,
k1; rep from * to last 3 sts, p1, k2.
ROW 17 P3, *k1, p9, k1, p1; rep from * to last 2 sts, p2.
ROW 18 K2, *p1, k1, p1, k2, yo, S2KP, yo, k2, p1, k1;
rep from * to last 3 sts, p1 k2.

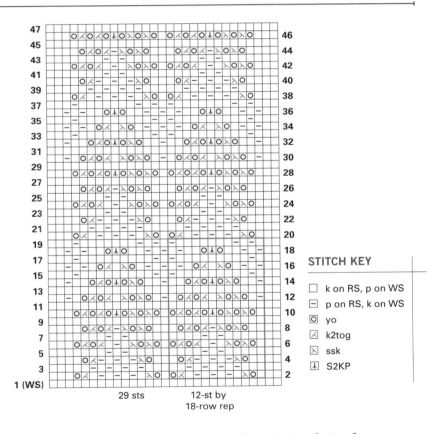

29 sts   12-st by
          18-row rep

ROW 19 P3, *k1, p7, [k1, p1] twice; rep from * to last 2 sts, p2.
ROWS 20–37 Rep rows 2–19 for stitch pattern once.
ROWS 38–47 Rep rows 2–11 once.
Bind off purlwise on WS. ■

STITCH KEY
☐ k on RS, p on WS
⊟ p on RS, k on WS
⊙ yo
⊠ k2tog
⊠ ssk
⊼ S2KP

75

SEED STITCH WITH FAGGOTING

(multiple of 7 sts plus 6)

Cast on 27 sts.
ROW 1 (RS) K1, p1, *yo, k2tog, [p1, k1] twice, p1;
rep from * to last 4 sts, yo, k2tog, p1, k1.
ROW 2 (WS) K1, p1, yo, p2tog, *[p1, k1] twice, p1, yo,
p2tog; rep from * to last 2 sts, p1, k1.
Rep rows 1 and 2 for seed stitch with faggoting pattern
11 times more—24 rows.
Bind off in pat. ∎

STITCH KEY

☐ k on RS, p on WS
⊟ p on RS, k on WS
⊡ yo
⊠ k2tog on RS,
   p2tog on WS

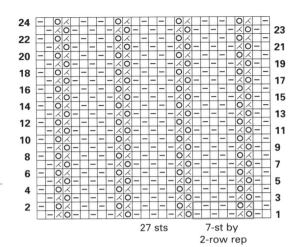

27 sts   7-st by
          2-row rep

LACY SHELLS ON SEED STITCH

SHELL STITCH

Insert RH needle into the front of the st 5 rows below the 3rd st on
LH needle and draw through a long loop. Leave loop on RH needle
and k1, make a 2nd loop into same st, k1, make a 3rd loop into
same st, k1, make a 4th loop into same st, k1, make a 5th st
into same st, k1, make a 6th loop into same st.

(multiple of 15 sts plus 2)
With A, cast on 32 sts.
PREPARATION ROW (WS) *K1, p1; rep from * to end.
ROWS 1, 3, AND 5 (RS) With B, *p1, k1; rep from * to end.
ROWS 2, 4, AND 6 With B, *k1, p1; rep from * to end.
ROW 7 With A, *work 9 sts in seed st, work shell st; rep from *
to last 2 sts, work 2 sts in seed st.
ROW 8 With A, k1, *(p2tog tbl) 3 times, p1, (p2tog) 3 times,
work 8 sts in seed st; rep from * to last st, p1.
ROWS 9, 11, AND 13 With B, rep row 1.
ROWS 10, 12, AND 14 With B, rep row 2.
ROW 15 With A, work 2 sts in seed st, *work shell st, work 9 sts
in seed st; rep from * to end.
ROW 16 With A, k1, *work 7 sts in seed st, *(p2tog tbl) 3 times,
p1, (p2tog) 3 times; rep to last st, k1.
ROWS 17–48 Rep rows 1–16 for stitch pattern twice.
ROWS 49–54 Rep rows 1–6 once, omitting shell sts.
Bind off. ∎

STITCH KEY

☐ k on RS, p on WS
⊟ p on RS, k on WS

▨ p2tog
⊠ p2tog tbl

shell st

COLOR KEY

▩ solid (A)
☐ color-changing (B)

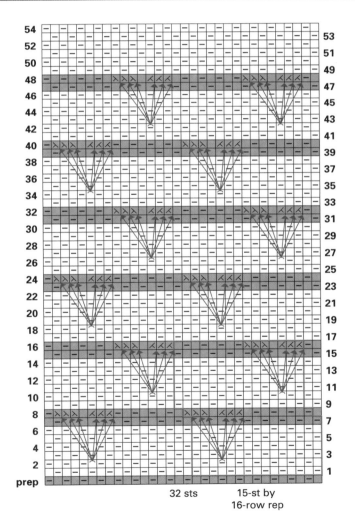

32 sts   15-st by
          16-row rep

project
portfolio

moss stitch cowl

A luxe alpaca-merino blend shows off the rich texture
of moss stitch in a simply stunning cowl.

■ ■ ■ ■

KNITTED MEASUREMENTS
Circumference 27½"/70cm
Height 11"/28cm

MATERIALS
• 2 3oz/85g skeins (each approx 100yd/90m) of
Long Island Livestock Co. *Worsted Weight* (alpaca/merino wool)
in Farmhouse White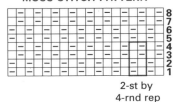

• Size 10½ (6.5mm) circular needle, 24"/60cm long,
OR SIZE TO OBTAIN GAUGE

• Stitch marker

GAUGE
14 sts and 24 rnds = 4"/10cm over moss st
using size 10½ (6.5mm) needle. TAKE TIME TO CHECK GAUGE.

MOSS STITCH
(over an even number of sts)
RNDS 1 AND 2 *K1, p1; rep from * around.
RNDS 3 AND 4 *P1, k1; rep from * around.
Rep rnds 1–4 for moss st.

COWL
Cast on 96 sts. Join, taking care not to twist sts.
Place marker for beg of rnd and sl marker every rnd.
Work in rib as foll:
RNDS 1–3 *P1, k1; rep from * around.
Work in moss st until piece measures 10"/25.5cm from beg.
Work 3 rnds in rib as before. Bind off loosely in rib. ■

MOSS STITCH PATTERN

2-st by
4-rnd rep

STITCH KEY

☐ k on RS, p on WS
⊟ p on RS, k on WS

● Design based on moss stitch on page 18.

striped wristers

Zigzag stripes and simple checks lend visual interest to a quick knit for chilly days.

■ ■ ▪ ▫ ▫

KNITTED MEASUREMENTS
Circumference 7"/18cm
Length 9½"/24cm

MATERIALS
• 1 1¾oz/50g ball (each approx 191yd/174m) of Rowan *Felted Tweed DK* (wool/alpaca/viscose) each in #177 Clay (A) and #194 Delft (B)

• One pair size 5 (3.75mm) needles
OR SIZE TO OBTAIN GAUGE

GAUGE
24 sts and 32 rows = 4"/10cm over check pattern
using size 5 (3.75mm) needles. TAKE TIME TO CHECK GAUGE.

NOTE
First and last st of every row is worked in St st
(k on RS, p on WS) with A.

WRISTERS
With A, cast on 42 sts.
ROW 1 (RS) *K2, p2; rep from *, end k2.
ROW 2 P2, *k2, p2; rep from * to end.

Rep rows 1 and 2 for k2, p2 rib for 4 more rows.

BEG ZIGZAG PAT
ROW 1 (RS) With A, k1, *k1, p1; rep from * to last st, k1.
ROW 2 With A, p1, *p1, k1; rep from * to last st, p1.
ROW 3 K1A, *k1B, (p1, k1, p1)A; rep from * to last st, k1A.
ROW 4 P1A, *p1B, k1A, (p1, k1)B; rep from * to last st, p1A.
ROW 5 K1A, *k1A, (p1, k1, p1)B; rep from * to last st, k1A.
ROW 6 P1A, *p1A, k1B, (p1, k1)A; rep from * to last st, p1A.
ROWS 7–18 Rep rows 1–6 twice more.

BEG CHECK PAT
ROW 19 (RS) With A, k1, *k1, p1; rep from * to last st, k1.
ROW 20 With A, p1, *p1, k1; rep from * to last st, p1.
ROW 21 K1A, *k1B, p1A; rep from * to last 2 sts, (p1, k1)A.
ROW 22 P2A, *k1B, p1A; rep from * to end.
ROWS 23–54 Rep rows 19–22 for 8 times.
ROWS 55–62 Rep rows 1–8 of zigzag pat once.
Cut B.
With A, work in k2, p2 rib as before for 6 rows.
Bind off in rib.

FINISHING
Block lightly. Beg at cast-on edge, sew seam for 5½"/14cm. Fasten off. Leave the next 1½"/4cm unsewn for thumb opening, then sew last 2½"/6cm. ■

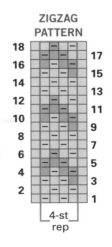

● Design based on zigzag stripes on page 32.

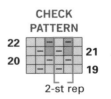

ZIGZAG PATTERN

4-st rep

CHECK PATTERN

2-st rep

STITCH KEY

☐ k on RS, p on WS
⊟ p on RS, k on WS

COLOR KEY

☐ Clay (A)
■ Delft (B)

zigzag pillow

Alternating seed stitch and stockinette chevrons lend dimension to a simple but bold design.

■ ■ ▨ ▨

KNITTED MEASUREMENTS
22"/56cm square

MATERIALS
• 4 3½oz/100g skeins (each approx 87yd/80m) of Rowan *Big Wool* (wool) in #001 White Hot (A) ⑥

• 2 skeins in #052 Steel Blue (B)

• One pair size 15 (10mm) needles
OR SIZE TO OBTAIN GAUGE

• One 22"/56cm pillow form

GAUGES
8 sts and 14 rows = 4"/10cm over seed st using size 15 (10mm) needles.

10 sts and 12 rows = 4"/10cm over zigzag pat using size 15 (10mm) needles.
TAKE TIME TO CHECK GAUGES.

SEED STITCH
(over an odd number of sts)
ROW 1 (RS) *K1, p1; rep from *, end k1.
ROW 2 K the purl sts and p the knit sts.
Rep row 2 for seed st.

NOTES
1. Work first and last st of every row with A in St st (k on RS, p on WS).
2. When changing colors, twist yarns on WS to prevent holes in work. Carry yarn not in use loosely across WS of work to prevent puckering.

FRONT
With A, cast on 53 sts. Knit 1 row, purl 1 row (rows 1 and 2 of chart). Cont in chart pat as foll:

BEG ZIGZAG PAT
ROW 3 (RS) K1A, *k1B, k4A, k1B, k4A; rep from * to last 2 sts, k1B, k1A.
ROW 4 P1A, (k1, p1)B, *p7A, (p1, k1, p1)B; rep from * to last st, p1A.
Cont to foll chart for zigzag pat as established through row 10, then rep rows 3–10 six times more, then work rows 11–13 once. Bind off with A on WS.

BACK
With A, cast on 45 sts. Work in seed st for 18"/46cm. Bind off in pat.

FINISHING
Block lightly. Sew front and back tog over 3 sides. Insert pillow form and sew rem side closed. ■

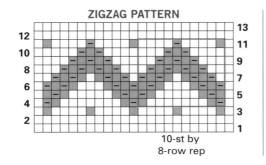

ZIGZAG PATTERN

10-st by
8-row rep

STITCH KEY
☐ k on RS, p on WS
⊟ p on RS, k on WS

COLOR KEY
☐ White Hot (A)
▨ Steel Blue (B)

● Design based on two-color chevron seed & stockinette on page 40.

slouchy hat

Seed stitch elevates a simple color pattern on a winter warmer topped with a fun fur pompom.

■ ■ ▨ ▨

SIZE
One size fits most

KNITTED MEASUREMENTS
Circumference 19½"/49.5cm
Length 10½"/26.5cm

MATERIALS
• 1 3½oz/100g skeins (approx 128yd/117m) of Cascade Yarns *128 Superwash* (merino wool) each in #1984 Light Yellow (A) and #821 Dark Yellow (B) (5)

• One pair each sizes 10 and 10½ (6 and 6.5mm) needles OR SIZE TO OBTAIN GAUGE

• Purchased faux fur pompom

• Stitch marker

• Yarn needle

GAUGE
16 sts and 20 rows = 4"/10cm over pat st using larger needles.
TAKE TIME TO CHECK GAUGE.

NOTE
When changing colors, twist yarns on WS to prevent holes in work. Carry yarn not in use loosely across WS of work to prevent puckering.

MISTAKE STITCH RIB
(multiple of 4 sts plus 3)
ROW 1 (RS) K1, *k2, p1, k1; rep from *, end k2.
ROW 2 K1, p1, *k3, p1; rep from *, end k1.
Rep rows 1 and 2 for mistake st rib.

SEED STITCH
(over an even number of sts)
ROW 1 (RS) *P1, k1; rep from * to end.
ROW 2 (WS) P the knit sts and k the purl sts.
Rep row 2 for seed st.

HAT
With smaller needles and A, cast on 79 sts. Work in mistake st rib for 3"/7.5cm, dec 1 st at end of last WS row—78 sts. Change to larger needles. Work in seed st for 2 rows.

BEG PAT ST CHART
ROW 1 (RS) P1A, *([k1, p1] twice)A, k1B, ([p1, k1] twice)A, p1B; rep from * to last 7 sts, end ([k1, p1] twice)A, k1B, (k1, p1)A.
ROW 2 (WS) (K1, p1)A, (k1, p1)B, (k1, p1, k1)A, *(p1, k1)B, (p1, k1, p1)A, (k1, p1)B, (k1, p1, k1)A; rep from * to last st, p1A.
Cont in chart pat as established through rnd 14, then rep rnds 1–14 once more, then rnds 1–8 once more.
Cut B and work with A only to end of hat.

SHAPE CROWN
DEC ROW 1 (RS) With A, p1, *k3tog tbl, p1; rep from * to last 5 sts, end k3tog, p1, k1—40 sts.
Work 1 row even in seed st.
DEC ROW 2 (RS) With A, *k2tog tbl, p2tog; rep from * to end—20 sts.
Cut yarn, leaving a long tail. Thread through 20 sts twice, pull tog tightly and secure end.

FINISHING
Sew back seam. Sew pompom to top of hat ■

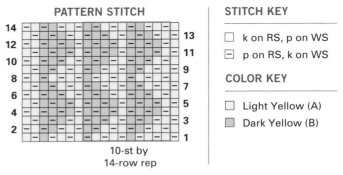

PATTERN STITCH

10-st by
14-row rep

STITCH KEY

☐ k on RS, p on WS
⊟ p on RS, k on WS

COLOR KEY

☐ Light Yellow (A)
▨ Dark Yellow (B)

● Design based on interlocking triangles on page 28.

striped long cowl

Feeling the blues? Wrap up in this cozy cowl that can be worn long for drama or doubled for warmth.

■ ■ ■ ■

KNITTED MEASUREMENTS
Width 10"/25.5cm
Length 50"/127cm

MATERIALS
• 1 8.82oz/250g skein (each approx 123yd/112m) of Cascade Yarns *Magnum* (wool) each in #9550 Dark Blue (A) and #9565B Light Blue (B) **7**

• One pair size 15 (10mm) needles
OR SIZE TO OBTAIN GAUGE

GAUGE
8 sts and 13 rows = 4"/10cm over stripe pat using size 15 (10mm) needles.
TAKE TIME TO CHECK GAUGE.

NOTE
Carry yarn not in use loosely along side of work to avoid cutting and weaving in ends.

STRIPE PATTERN
(over an odd number of sts)
ROW 1 (RS) With A, knit.
ROW 2 With A, k1, purl to last st, k1.
ROWS 3–6 With B, k1, *p1, k1; rep from * to end.
Rep rows 1–6 for stripe pat.

COWL
With A, cast on 21 sts. Work in stripe pat until piece measures approx 50"/127cm, end with a pat row 6. Bind off in pat with A.

FINISHING
Block lightly. Sew cast-on and bound-off edges tog. ■

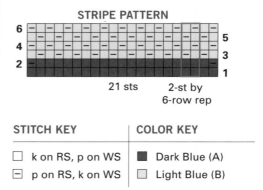

STRIPE PATTERN

6
4
2
5
3
1

21 sts   2-st by
6-row rep

STITCH KEY

☐ k on RS, p on WS

⊟ p on RS, k on WS

COLOR KEY

■ Dark Blue (A)

☐ Light Blue (B)

● Design based on seed & stockinette stripes on page 62.

two-way stripe bag

Can't get enough of stripes? Knit them going in two directions in one fun project.

■ ■ ▨ ▨

KNITTED MEASUREMENTS
Width 14"/35.5cm
Length 15¾"/40cm

MATERIALS
• 2 1¾oz/50g balls (each approx 155yd/140m) of Classic Elite Yarns *Firefly* (viscose/linen) in #7757 Chicory (A) ②

• 1 ball in #7703 Light Gray (B)

• One pair size 4 (3.5mm) needles OR SIZE TO OBTAIN GAUGE

GAUGES
22 sts and 40 rows = 4"/10cm over horizontal stripe pat using size 4 (3.5mm) needles.

26 sts and 28 rows = 4"/10cm over vertical stripe pat using size 4 (3.5mm) needles.
TAKE TIME TO CHECK GAUGES.

NOTES
1. Bag is made in two pieces, with each side in a different stitch pattern. Either side can be used as the front.
2. When working the horizontal stripe pat, carry color not in use loosely along side of work to avoid cutting and weaving in ends.
3. When changing colors on the vertical stripe pat, twist yarns on WS to prevent holes in work. Carry yarn not in use loosely across WS of work to prevent puckering.

FRONT
With A, cast on 87 sts.

BEG VERTICAL STRIPE PAT
ROW 1 (RS) *(P1, k1, p1)A, (k1, p1, k1)B; rep from * to last 3 sts, (p1, k1, p1)A.
ROW 2 (WS) *(K1, p1, k1)A, (p1, k1, p1)B; rep from * to last 3 sts, (k1, p1, k1)A. Cont in seed st and colors as established until piece measures approx 15¼"/38.5cm from beg. Cut B.
With A only, work 4 rows in seed st as established. Bind off in pat.

BACK
With A, cast on 79 sts.

BEG HORIZONTAL STRIPE PATTERN
ROWS 1 AND 3 (RS) With A, *p1, k1; rep from * to end.
ROWS 2 AND 4 (WS) With A, *k1, p1; rep from * to end.
ROWS 5–8 With B, rep rows 1–4. Rep rows 1–8 until piece measures 15¾"/40cm from beg. Bind off in pat.

FINISHING
Block lightly to measurements. Sew cast-on edges of both pieces tog, then sew side seams.

STRAP
With A, cast on 5 sts.
Work in seed st for 24"/61cm or desired length. Bind off. Sew ends of strap to inside of bag at both side seams. ■

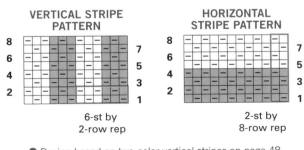

VERTICAL STRIPE PATTERN

6-st by
2-row rep

HORIZONTAL STRIPE PATTERN

2-st by
8-row rep

● Design based on two-color vertical stripes on page 48.

STITCH KEY

☐ k on RS, p on WS

⊟ p on RS, k on WS

COLOR KEY

▨ Chicory (A)

☐ Light Gray (B)

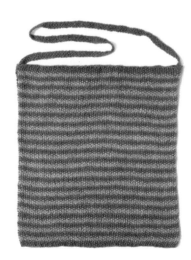

striped cowl

The texture of seed stitch adds depth and sophistication to the classic look of stripes.

■ ■ ◼ ◻

KNITTED MEASUREMENTS
Circumference 28"/71cm
Height 10"/25.5cm

MATERIALS
• 1 3oz/85g skein (each approx 100yd/90m) of Long Island Livestock Co. *Worsted Weight* (alpaca/merino wool) each in Farmhouse White (A) and Classic Denim (B)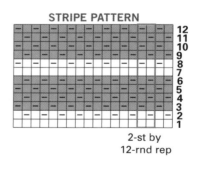

• Size 10½ (6.5mm) circular needle, 24"/60cm long, OR SIZE TO OBTAIN GAUGE

• Stitch marker

GAUGE
14 sts and 22 rnds = 4"/10cm over stripe pat using size 10½ (6.5mm) needle. TAKE TIME TO CHECK GAUGE.

NOTE
Carry yarn not in use loosely at beg of rnd to avoid cutting and weaving in ends.

STRIPE PATTERN
(over an even number of sts)
RND 1 With A, knit.
RND 2 With A, *p1, k1; rep from * around.
RND 3 With B, *k1, p1; rep from * around.
RND 4 With B, *p1, k1; rep from * around.
RNDS 5 AND 6 Rep rnds 3 and 4.
RND 7 With A, knit.
RND 8 With A, *k1, p1; rep from * around.
RNDS 9 AND 11 With B, *p1, k1; rep from * around
RNDS 10 AND 12 With B, *k1, p1; rep from * around.
Rep rnds 1–12 for stripe pat.

COWL
With A, cast on 96 sts. Join, taking care not to twist sts. Place marker for beg of rnd and sl marker every rnd.
Work in k1, p1 rib as foll:
RNDS 1–3 *K1, p1; rep from * around.
Rep rnds 1–12 of stripe pat until there are 8 B stripes, end with a pat rnd 12—piece measures approx 9"/23cm from beg. Cut B.
With A, knit 1 rnd.
Work 3 rnds in k1, p1 rib as before. Bind off loosely in rib. ■

STRIPE PATTERN

```
                              12
                              11
                              10
                               9
                               8
                               7
                               6
                               5
                               4
                               3
                               2
                               1
```

2-st by
12-rnd rep

STITCH KEY	COLOR KEY
☐ k on RS, p on WS	☐ Farmhouse White (A)
⊟ p on RS, k on WS	▨ Classic Denim (B)

● Design based on seed & stockinette stripes on page 62.

cropped pullover

A striped and structured top is a great piece for layering or pairing with a high waist.

■ ■ ■ ■

SIZES
Sized for Small, Medium, Large, and X-Large and shown in size Small.

MATERIALS
• 3 (3, 4, 4) 3½oz/100g hanks each (each approx 137yd/125m) of Manos del Uruguay/Fairmount Fibers *Wool Clasica* (wool) in #54 Brick (A) and #28 Copper (B) (4)

• One pair size 8 (5mm) needles OR SIZE TO OBTAIN GAUGE

• Size 8 (5mm) circular needle, 16"/40cm long

• 2 stitch holders

• Stitch marker

KNITTED MEASUREMENTS
Bust 36 (40, 44, 48)"/91.5 (101.5, 111.5, 122)cm
Length 15½ (16½, 17, 18)"/39.5 (42, 43, 45.5)cm
Upper arm 14½ (14½, 15, 15¾)"/37 (37, 38, 40)cm

GAUGE
13 sts and 24 rows = 4"/10cm over seed st using size 8 (5mm) needles.
TAKE TIME TO CHECK GAUGE.

SEED STITCH
(over an odd number of sts)
ROW 1 (RS) K1, *p1, k1; rep from * to end.
ROW 2 P the knit sts and k the purl sts.
Rep row 2 for seed st.

BACK
With straight needles and A, cast on 59 (65, 71, 79) sts.

BEG SEED STITCH STRIPE PATTERN
ROW 1 (RS) With A, k1, *p1, k1; rep from * to end.
ROWS 2 AND 3 Rep row 1.
ROWS 4 AND 5 With B, rep row 1.
Rep rows 2–5 for seed st stripe pat until piece measures 8½ (9, 9, 9½)"/21.5 (23, 23, 24)cm from beg, end with a WS row.

ARMHOLE SHAPING
Bind off 3 (3, 4, 5) sts at beg of next 2 rows.
NEXT (DEC) ROW (RS) K2tog tbl, work in pat to last 2 sts, k2tog.
Rep dec row every other row 2 (3, 3, 5) times more—47 (51, 55, 57) sts.
Work even in pat until armhole measures 7 (7½, 8, 8½)"/18 (19, 20.5, 21.5)cm.
Bind off 11 (13, 14, 15) sts at beg of next 2 rows, place rem 25 (25, 27, 27) sts on a stitch holder for back neck.

FRONT
Work as for back until armhole measures 4½ (5, 5½, 6)"/11.5 (12.5, 14, 15)cm, end with a WS row.

NECK SHAPING
NEXT ROW (RS) Work 18 (20, 22, 23) sts, place next 11 sts on a stitch holder, join a 2nd ball of yarn and work to end of row.
Working both sides at once, bind off 2 sts from each neck edge twice, then dec 1 st every other row 3 (3, 4, 4) times—11 (13, 14, 15) sts rem each side.
Work even in pat until piece measures same as back to shoulder.
Bind off sts each side.

cropped pullover

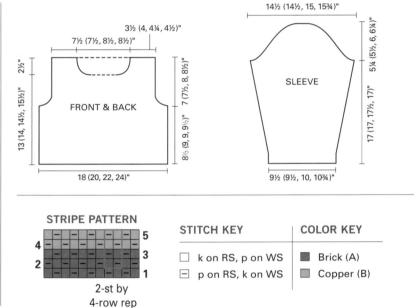

STRIPE PATTERN

2-st by
4-row rep

STITCH KEY	COLOR KEY
□ k on RS, p on WS	■ Brick (A)
⊟ p on RS, k on WS	▨ Copper (B)

SLEEVES

With straight needles and A, cast on 31 (31, 33, 35) sts. Work in seed st stripe pat as for back until 8 rows are complete.
NEXT ROW (RS) Inc 1 st at each side, working inc'd sts into pat. Cont in pat as established and rep inc row every 10th row 3 times more, then every 14th row 4 times—47 (47, 49, 51) sts.
Work even until piece measures 17 (17, 17½, 17½)"/43 (43, 44.5, 44.5)cm from beg, end with a WS row.

CAP SHAPING
Bind off 3 (3, 4, 5) sts at beg of next 2 rows, then dec 1 st at each side of every other row 14 (14, 15, 15) times.
Work 0 (2, 2, 4) rows even.
Bind off 4 (4, 3, 3) sts at beg of next 2 rows, bind off rem 5 sts.

FINISHING

Block pieces lightly to measurements. Sew shoulder seams.

NECKBAND
With RS facing, circular needle and A, beg at left shoulder seam and pick up and k 12 (12, 13, 13) sts along left front neck edge, k11 from front neck holder, pick up and k 12 (12, 13, 13) sts along right front neck edge, k25 (25, 27, 27) from back neck holder—60 (60, 64, 64) sts. Join and place marker for beg of rnd.
RND 1 *K1, p1; rep from * to end.
RND 2 *P1, k1; rep from * to end.
Rep rnd 1 once more, then bind off loosely in pat.
Set in sleeves. Sew side and sleeve seams. ■

diamond check hat

A fur pompom makes this classic hat look luxe,
or leave it off for a great unisex option.

■ ■ ▦ ▨

SIZE
One fits most

KNITTED MEASUREMENTS
Circumference 20"/51cm
Length 8"/20.5cm (with brim folded back)

MATERIALS
• 2 1¾oz/50g skeins (each approx 136yd/125m)
of MountainTop by Classic Elite Yarns *Chalet*
(alpaca/bamboo viscose) in #7477 Dark Gray (A) ⑤

• 1 skein in #7403 Light Gray (B)

• Sizes 9 and 10 (5.5 and 6mm) circular needles, 16"
or 20"/40cm or 50cm long, OR SIZE TO OBTAIN GAUGE

• Purchased faux fur pompom

• Stitch marker

• Yarn needle

GAUGE
18 sts and 24 rnds = 4"/10cm over check pat using larger
needle. TAKE TIME TO CHECK GAUGE.

NOTE
When changing colors, twist yarns on WS to prevent
holes in work. Carry yarn not in use loosely across WS of
work to prevent puckering.

CHECK PATTERN

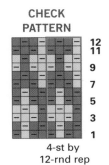

12
11
9
7
5
3
1

4-st by
12-rnd rep

STITCH KEY	COLOR KEY
☐ k on RS, p on WS	■ Dark Gray (A)
⊟ p on RS, k on WS	▨ Light Gray (B)

● Design based on broken crosses
starting with a knit on page 44.

SEED STITCH
(over an even number of sts in the round)
RND 1 (RS) *K1, p1; rep from * around.
RND 2 *P1, k1; rep from * around.
Rep rnds 1 and 2 for seed st in the round.

CHECK PATTERN
(over a multiple of 4 sts in the round)
RND 1 *(K1, p1)A, k1B, p1A; rep from * around.
RND 2 *(P1, k1)A, p1B, k1A; rep from * around.
RND 3 *K1A, (p1, k1, p1)B; rep from * around.
RND 4 *P1A, (k1, p1, k1)B; rep from * around.
RND 5 Rep rnd 1.
RND 6 Rep rnd 2.
RND 7 *K1B, (p1, k1, p1)A; rep from * around.
RND 8 *P1B, (k1, p1, k1)A; rep from * around.
RND 9 *(K1, p1)B, k1A, p1B; rep from * around.
RND 10 *(P1, k1)B, p1A, k1B; rep from * around.
RNDS 11 AND 12 Rep rnds 7 and 8.
Rep rnds 1–12 for check pat.

HAT
With smaller circular needle and A, cast on 92 sts.
Join, taking care not to twist sts. Place marker for beg of
rnd and sl marker every rnd.
NEXT RND *K1, p1; rep from * around.
Rep last rnd for k1, p1 rib until piece measures 2½"/6.5cm
from beg. Change to larger needle.

BEG SEED STITCH
Beg with a pat rnd 2, work in seed st in the round for
2½"/6.5cm more, ending with a pat rnd 2.

BEG CHECK PAT
Work rnd 1–12 of check pat twice, then work rnds 1–6 once
more. Cut B and work with A only to end of hat.

SHAPE CROWN
DEC RND 1 *K3tog, p1; rep from * around—46 sts.
DEC RND 2 *P2tog, k2tog; rep from *, end p2tog—23 sts.
Cut yarn, leaving a long tail. Thread through 23 sts twice,
pull tog tightly and secure end.

FINISHING
Sew pompom to top of hat. ■

checkerboard cowl

Seed stitch checks and a tall, cozy shape make a playful accessory that'll keep out the chill.

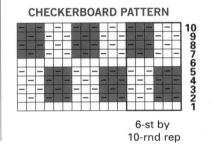

CHECKERBOARD PATTERN

6-st by
10-rnd rep

STITCH KEY

☐ k on RS, p on WS

⊟ p on RS, k on WS

COLOR KEY

☐ Farmhouse White (A)

■ Espresso (B)

● Design based on checkerboard pattern on page 50.

KNITTED MEASUREMENTS
Circumference 25½"/64.5cm
Height 7"/18cm

MATERIALS
• 1 3oz/85g skein (each approx 100yd/90m) of Long Island Livestock Co. *Worsted Weight* (alpaca/merino wool) each in Farmhouse White (A) and Espresso (B) ④

• Size 10½ (6.5mm) circular needle, 24"/60cm long, OR SIZE TO OBTAIN GAUGE

• Stitch marker

GAUGE
15 sts and 18 rnds = 4"/10cm over checkerboard pat using size 10½ (6.5mm) needle. TAKE TIME TO CHECK GAUGE.

NOTE
When changing colors, twist yarns on WS to prevent holes in work. Carry yarn not in use loosely across WS of work to prevent puckering.

CHECKERBOARD PATTERN
(over a multiple of 6 sts)
RND 1 With A, knit.
RNDS 2 AND 4 *(P1, k1, p1)B, (k1, p1 k1)A; rep from * around.
RNDS 3 AND 5 *(K1, p1, k1)B, (p1, k1 p1)A; rep from * around.
RND 6 With A, knit.
RNDS 7 AND 9 *(P1, k1, p1)A, (k1, p1 k1)B; rep from * around.
RNDS 8 AND 10 *(K1, p1, k1)A, (p1, k1 p1)B; rep from * around.
Rep rnds 1–10 for checkerboard pat.

COWL
With A, cast on 96 sts. Join, taking care not to twist sts.
Place marker for beg of rnd and sl marker every rnd.
Work in k1, p1 rib as foll:
RNDS 1–3 *K1, p1; rep from * around.

BEG CHECKERBOARD PATTERN
Work rnds 1–10 of checkerboard pat 3 times. Cut B.
With A, knit 1 rnd.
Work 3 rnds in k1, p1 rib as before. Bind off loosely in rib. ■

chunky throw

A slip stitch pattern pops in super-bulky wool that knits up fast into a pretty throw.

■ ■ ▨ ▨

KNITTED MEASUREMENTS
35 x 42"/89 x 106.5cm

MATERIALS
• 6 3½oz/100g hanks (each approx 71yd/65m) of Tahki Yarns/Tahki•Stacy Charles *Big Montana* (wool) in #201 White 🎱

• Size 19 (15mm) circular needle, 48"/122cm long, OR SIZE TO OBTAIN GAUGE

GAUGE
8 sts and 15 rows = 4"/10cm
over sl st pat using size 19 (15mm) needles.
TAKE TIME TO CHECK GAUGE.

NOTES
1. Keep first and last 5 sts in seed st.
2. Circular needle is used to accommodate the large number of sts. Do *not* join.

SLIP STITCH PATTERN
(multiple of 6 sts plus 4)
ROW 1 (RS) Knit.
ROW 2 Purl.
ROW 3 K1, *sl 2 wyib, [p1, k1] twice; rep from *, end sl 2 wyib, k1.
ROW 4 K1, *sl 2 wyif, [k1, p1] twice; rep from *, end sl 2 wyif, k1.
ROWS 5 AND 6 Rep rows 3 and 4.
ROWS 7 AND 8 Rep rows 1 and 2.
ROW 9 [P1, k1] twice, *sl 2 wyib, [p1, k1] twice; rep from * to end.
ROW 10 [K1, p1] twice, *sl 2 wyif, [k1, p1] twice; rep from * to end.
ROWS 11 AND 12 Rep rows 9 and 10.
Rep rows 1–12 for sl st pat.

THROW
Cast on 68 sts. Work in seed st as foll:
ROW 1 (RS) *P1, k1; rep from * to end.
ROW 2 K the purl sts and p the knit sts.
ROWS 3–6 Rep rows 1 and 2 twice.
Keeping 5 sts each side in seed st as established, work center 58 sts in sl st pat, until piece measures approx 37"/94cm from beg, ending with pat row 8.
Work 6 rows in seed st over all sts as before.
Bind off in pat.

FINISHING
Block lightly to measurements. ■

SLIP STITCH PATTERN

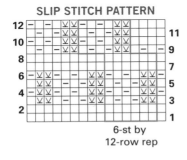

6-st by
12-row rep

STITCH KEY

☐ k on RS, p on WS   ☑ slip 1 wyib on RS,
⊟ p on RS, k on WS   slip 1 wyif on WS

● Design based on staggered slip stitch checks on page 66.

v-neck short sleeve pullover

This tunic's modern chunky look is balanced
by short sleeves and a deep V-neck.

■ ■ ▩ ▩

SIZES
Sized for Small, Medium, Large, X-Large, and XX-Large.
Shown in size Small.

KNITTED MEASUREMENTS
• Bust 38 (40, 43½, 45, 49)"/96.5
(101.5, 110.5, 114, 124.5)cm

• Length 28½ (29½, 30½, 31, 31½)"/72.5
(75, 77.5, 78.5, 80)cm

• Upper arm 13 (14, 15, 16, 17)"/33 (35.5, 38, 40.5, 43)cm

MATERIALS
• 9 (10, 11, 12, 13) 3½oz/100g skeins
(each approx 87yd/80m) of Debbie Bliss/KFI *Roma*
(merino wool/alpaca) in #09 Duck Egg 🔵6️⃣

• One pair size 15 (10mm) needles OR SIZE TO OBTAIN GAUGE

• One size 15 (10mm) circular needle, 29"/74cm long

• Stitch markers

• Stitch holders

GAUGE
9 sts and 16 rows = 4"/10cm over
seed st pat using size 15 (10mm) needles.
TAKE TIME TO CHECK GAUGE.

SEED STITCH PATTERN
(over an odd number of sts)
ROW 1 (RS) K1, *p1, k1; rep from * to end.
ROW 2 K the purl and p the knit sts.
Rep row 2 for seed st pat.

BACK
Cast on 43 (45, 49, 51, 55) sts.
ROW 1 (RS) K1, *p1, k1; rep from * to end.
ROW 2 (WS) P1, *k1, p1; rep from * to end.

Rep rows 1 and 2 for k1, p1 rib until piece measures
2"/5cm from beg. Then, work in seed st until piece
measures 18"/45.5cm from beg.

BEG SLEEVES
Cast on 8 sts at beg of next 2 rows—59 (61, 65, 67, 71) sts.
Cont in seed st until sleeve edge measures 6½
(7, 7½, 8, 8½)"/16.5 (18, 19, 20.5, 21.5)cm.

SHOULDER SHAPING
Bind off 1 st at beg of next 8 (10, 10, 10, 10) rows, 2 sts at
beg of next 2 (2, 4, 4, 2) rows, 3 sts at beg of next 4 (4, 4, 4, 6)
rows, 8 (8, 8, 8, 9) sts at beg of next 2 rows.
Bind off 19 (19, 19, 21, 21) sts for back neck.

v-neck short sleeve pullover

FRONT
Work as for back until piece measures 15 (16, 16, 17, 17)"/38 (40.5, 40.5, 43, 43)cm from beg.

NECK SHAPING
NEXT ROW (RS) Work 21 (22, 24, 25, 27) sts in pat, place center st on st holder or safety pin, join 2nd ball of yarn and work in pat to end.
Working both sides at same time with separate balls of yarn, dec 1 st at each neck edge on 3rd row, then every 4th row 3 (3, 3, 4, 4) times more, then every 6th row 3 times, then every 4th row twice, AT SAME TIME, when piece measures 18"/45.5cm from beg, work sleeve and shoulder shaping as for back.

FINISHING
Block pieces to measurements. Sew shoulder seams.

SLEEVE BANDS
With RS facing, pick up and k 33 (35, 39, 41, 45) sts evenly around sleeve edge. Beg with a p1, work in k1, p1 rib for 5 rows. Bind off in rib.
Sew side and sleeve seams.

NECKBAND
With RS facing and circular needle, pick up and k 20 (20, 20, 22, 22) sts along back neck, 38 (40, 40, 42, 42) sts along left front neck, pm, k center st from holder, pm, pick up and k 38 (40, 40, 42, 42) sts along right front—97 (101, 101, 107, 107) sts. Join and place marker for beg of rnd.
NEXT RND Work in k1, p1 rib to 2 sts before first marker, ssk, sl marker, k1, k2tog, rib to end.
Rep last rnd 4 times more. Bind off rem sts in rib, working decreases at center neck as before. ■

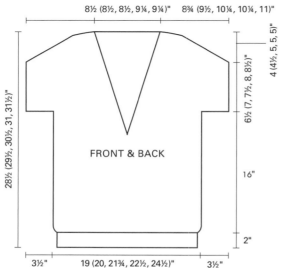

8½ (8½, 8½, 9¼, 9¼)"   8¾ (9½, 10¼, 10¼, 11)"

4 (4½, 5, 5, 5)"

6½ (7, 7½, 8, 8½)"

28½ (29½, 30½, 31, 31½)"

FRONT & BACK

16"

2"

3½"   19 (20, 21¾, 22½, 24½)"   3½"

graphic pillow trio

A mix of bold patterns is a rustic but modern accent for any decor.

Mini Diamonds Pillow
■ ■ ▨ ▨

KNITTED MEASUREMENTS
22"/56cm square

MATERIALS
• 4 3½oz/100g skeins (approx 87yd/80m) of
Rowan *Big Wool* (wool) in #001 White Hot (A) 🌕

• 2 skeins in #021 Ice Blue (B)

• One pair size 15 (10mm) needles OR SIZE TO OBTAIN GAUGE

• One 22"/56cm pillow form

GAUGES
8 sts and 14 rows = 4"/10cm over seed st
using size 15 (10mm) needles.

10 sts and 11 rows = 4"/10cm over mini diamonds pat using size
15 (10mm) needles. TAKE TIME TO CHECK GAUGES.

NOTE
When changing colors, twist yarns on WS to prevent
holes in work. Carry yarn not in use loosely across WS of
work to prevent puckering.

SEED STITCH
(over an odd number of sts)
ROW 1 (RS) *P1, k1; rep from * to end, p1.
ROW 2 K the purl sts and p the knit sts.
Rep row 2 for seed st.

FRONT
With A, cast on 55 sts.

■ Clockwise
from top:
Mini Diamonds
Pillow, Moss
Stitch Striped
Pillow, Narrow
Zigzag Pillow

BEG MINI DIAMONDS PAT
ROWS 1 AND 2 With A, *p1, k1; rep from *, end p1.
ROW 3 (RS) *(P1, k1, p1)A, k1B; rep from * to last 3 sts,
(p1, k1, p1)A.
ROW 4 (P1, k1)A, *(p1, k1, p1)B, (k1, p1, k1, p1, k1)A;
rep from * to last 2 sts, (k1, p1)A.
Cont in chart as established through row 10, then rep rows 3–10
six times more, then work rows 11–13 once.
Bind off in pat with A on WS.

BACK
With A, cast on 45 sts. Work in seed st for 18"/46cm.
Bind off in pat.

FINISHING
Block lightly. Sew front and back tog over 3 sides. Insert pillow
form and sew rem side closed. ■

MINI DIAMONDS PATTERN

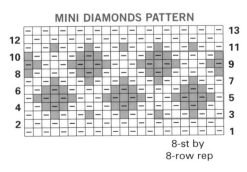

8-st by
8-row rep

STITCH KEY	COLOR KEY
☐ k on RS, p on WS	☐ White Hot (A)
⊟ p on RS, k on WS	▨ Ice Blue (B)

● Design based on mini diamonds on page 52.

graphic pillow trio

Narrow Zigzag Pillow
■ ■ ▪ ▪

KNITTED MEASUREMENTS
18"/46cm square (after finishing)

MATERIALS
• 3 1¾oz/250g skeins (each approx 137yd/125m) of Fibra Natura *Flax* (linen) in #11 Adriatic (A) ▣❸

• 2 skeins in #14 White (B)

• One pair size 6 (4mm) needles OR SIZE TO OBTAIN GAUGE

• One 18"/46cm pillow form

• Stitch markers

GAUGES
19 sts and 23 rows = 4"/10cm over zigzag pat using size 6 (4mm) needles and 2 strands of yarn held tog.

20 sts and 28 rows = 4"/10cm over St st using size 6 (4mm) needles and 1 strand of yarn.
TAKE TIME TO CHECK GAUGES.

NOTES
1. Use two strands held tog for the front and one strand for the back.
2. Keep 2 sts each side in seed st with B.

3. The front and back pieces are slightly smaller than 18"/46cm and will stretch to fit the pillow form for a snug fit.

SEED STITCH
(over an odd number of sts)
ROW 1 (RS) *p1, k1; rep from *, end p1.
ROW 2 K the purl sts and p the knit sts.
Rep row 2 for seed st.

FRONT
With 2 strands of B, cast on 85 sts.
Beg with a RS row, work in seed st for 2 rows.

BEG ZIGZAG PATTERN
ROW 1 (RS) (P1, k1)B, place marker (pm), *(p1, k1, p1)A, (k1, p1, k1)B; rep from * to last 5 sts, (p1, k1, p1) A, pm, (k1, p1)B.
ROW 2 (WS) (P1, k1)B, slip marker (sm), (p1, k1)A, p1B, *(k1, p1)B, (k1, p1, k1) A, p1B; rep from * to marker, sm, (k1, p1)B.
Cont in seed st and foll chart for zigzag pat, keeping 2 sts each side in B until piece measures approx 17½"/44.5cm from beg, end with a WS row. With B, work in seed st over all sts for 2 rows.
Bind off in pat with B.

BACK
With 1 strand of A, cast on 83 sts. Work in St st (k on RS, p on WS) for 17½"/44.5cm. Bind off loosely.

FINISHING
Block lightly. Sew front and back tog over 3 sides. Insert pillow form and sew rem side closed. ■

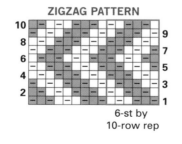

ZIGZAG PATTERN

6-st by
10-row rep

STITCH KEY		COLOR KEY	
☐	k on RS, p on WS	▨	2 strands Adriatic (A)
⊟	p on RS, k on WS	☐	2 strands White (B)

● Design based on zigzag seed & stockinette on page 64.

graphic pillow trio

Moss Stitch Striped Pillow
■ ■ ■ ■

KNITTED MEASUREMENTS
18"/46cm square (after finishing)

MATERIALS
• 3 1¾oz/250g skeins (each approx 137yd/125m) of Fibra Natura *Flax* (linen) in #12 Tarragon (A) (3)

• 2 skeins in #14 White (B)

• One pair size 6 (4mm) needles OR SIZE TO OBTAIN GAUGE

• One 18"/46cm pillow form

GAUGES
18 sts and 28 rows = 4"/10cm over moss st using size 6 (4mm) needles and 2 strands of yarn held tog.

20 sts and 28 rows = 4"/10cm over St st using size 6 (4mm) needles and 1 strand of yarn. TAKE TIME TO CHECK GAUGES.

NOTES
1. Use two strands held tog for the front and one strand for the back.
2. The front and back pieces are slightly smaller than 18"/46cm and will stretch to fit the pillow form for a snug fit.

MOSS STITCH
(over an odd number of sts)
ROW 1 (RS) *K1, p1; rep from *, end k1.
ROWS 2 AND 4 K the knit sts and p the purl sts.
ROW 3 *P1, k1; rep from *, end p1.
Rep rows 1–4 for moss st.

FRONT
With 2 strands of B, cast on 77 sts.

BEG MOSS STITCH STRIPES
ROWS 1–6 With 2 strands B, work in moss st.
ROWS 7–12 With 2 strands A, work in moss st.
Rep rows 1–12 for pat until 11 B stripes have been worked. Bind off in pat with B.

BACK
With 1 strand of A, cast on 85 sts. Work in St st (k on RS, p on WS) for 17½"/44.5cm. Bind off loosely.

FINISHING
Block lightly. Sew front and back tog over 3 sides. Insert pillow form and sew rem side closed. ■

MOSS ST STRIPE

2-st by
12-row rep

STITCH KEY	COLOR KEY
□ k on RS, p on WS	▨ 2 strands Tarragon (A)
⊟ p on RS, k on WS	□ 2 strands White (B)

● Design based on two-row striped moss stitch on page 58.

windowpane & diamonds pillows

Graphic patterns knit up quick and look chic in bulky wool.

Windowpane Pillow
■ ■ ■ ■

KNITTED MEASUREMENTS
18"/46cm square

MATERIALS
• 2 3½oz/100g skeins (each approx 87yd/80m)
of Rowan *Big Wool* (wool) in #001 White Hot (A)

• 1 skein in #021 Ice Blue (B) 🔢

• One pair size 15 (10mm) needles OR SIZE TO OBTAIN GAUGE

• One 18"/46cm pillow form

GAUGES
8 sts and 12 rows = 4"/10cm over seed st
using size 15 (10mm) needles.

10 sts and 9 rows = 4"/10cm over windowpane pat
using size 15 (10mm) needles. TAKE TIME TO CHECK GAUGES.

NOTE
When changing colors, twist yarns on WS to prevent
holes in work. Carry yarn not in use loosely across WS of
work to prevent puckering.

SEED STITCH
(over an odd number of sts)

■ From top:
Windowpane
Pillow,
Diamonds
Pillow

ROW 1 (RS) *K1, p1; rep from * to end, k1.
Rep row 1 for seed st.

FRONT
With B, cast on 45 sts.

BEG WINDOWPANE PAT
ROWS 1 AND 2 With B, *k1, p1; rep from *, end k1.
ROWS 3–8 (K1, p1)A, k1B, *(p1, k1, p1)A, k1B;
rep from * to last 2 sts, (p1, k1)A.
ROWS 9 AND 10 Rep rows 1 and 2.
ROWS 11–16 (K1, p1, k1, p1)A, *k1B, (p1, k1, p1)A;
rep from * to last 5 sts, k1B, (p1, k1, p1, k1)A.
Rep rows 1–16 for windowpane pat once more, then
rep rows 1–10 once.
Bind off in pat with B.

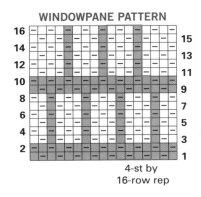

WINDOWPANE PATTERN

4-st by
16-row rep

STITCH KEY	COLOR KEY
☐ k on RS, p on WS	☐ White Hot (A)
⊟ p on RS, k on WS	▨ Ice Blue (B)

● Design based on staggered windowpane on page 30.

windowpane & diamonds pillows

BACK
With A, cast on 37 sts. Work in seed st for 18"/46cm.
Bind off in pat.

FINISHING
Block lightly. Sew front and back tog over 3 sides. Insert
pillow form and sew rem side closed. ■

Diamonds Pillow
■ ■ ▪ ▪

KNITTED MEASUREMENTS
18"/46cm square

MATERIALS
• 2 3½oz/100g skeins (each approx 87yd/80m) of
Rowan *Big Wool* (wool) in #001 White Hot (A) and
1 skein in #021 Ice Blue (B) ⑥⑤

• One pair size 15 (10mm) needles OR SIZE TO OBTAIN GAUGE

• One 18"/46cm pillow form

GAUGES
8 sts and 10 rows = 4"/10cm over moss st
using size 15 (10mm) needles.

10 sts and 12 rows = 4"/10cm over diamond pat
using size 15 (10mm) needles. TAKE TIME TO CHECK GAUGES.

NOTE
When changing colors, twist yarns on WS to prevent
holes in work. Carry yarn not in use loosely across WS of
work to prevent puckering.

MOSS STITCH
(over an odd number of sts)
ROW 1 (RS) *P1, k1; rep from *, end p1.
ROWS 2 AND 4 K the knit sts and p the purl sts.
ROW 3 *K1, p1; rep from *, end k1.
Rep rows 1–4 for moss st.

FRONT
With A, cast on 45 sts.

BEG DIAMOND PATTERN
ROW 1 (RS) With A, *p1, k1; rep from * to last st, p1.
ROW 2 With A, k the knit sts and p the purl sts.
ROW 3 ([K1, p1] twice)A, *k1B, ([p1, k1] twice, p1)A; rep from *
to last 5 sts, k1B, ([p1, k1] twice)A.
ROW 4 Cont in moss st, matching colors from previous row.
Cont in chart pat as established until rows 3–14 of diamond pat
have been worked twice, then work rows 15–24 once.
Bind off in pat with A.

BACK
With A, cast on 37 sts. Work in moss st for 18"/46cm.
Bind off in pat.

FINISHING
Block lightly. Sew front and back tog over 3 sides. Insert pillow
form and sew rem side closed. ■

DIAMOND PATTERN

6-st by
12-row rep

STITCH KEY

☐ k on RS, p on WS

⊟ p on RS, k on WS

COLOR KEY

☐ White Hot (A)

▨ Ice Blue (B)

● Design based on diamonds & dots on page 42.

open squares cowl

Seed stitch strikes a perfect balance with negative space in a unique, eye-catching accessory.

■ ■ ■ ■

KNITTED MEASUREMENTS
Width 9"/23cm
Length 30"/76cm

MATERIALS
• 1 4oz/115g skein (approx 251yd/230m) of Fyberspates *Vivacious DK* (merino wool) in #804 Sunshine

• One pair size 6 (4mm) needles OR SIZE TO OBTAIN GAUGE

GAUGE
22 sts and 30 rows = 4"/10cm over seed st
using size 6 (4mm) needles. TAKE TIME TO CHECK GAUGE.

NOTES
1. When casting on sts for the open squares pattern, use the twisted loop cast-on.
2. The entire cowl is worked in seed stitch. As this pattern is reversible, place a marker on the right side of the work.

SEED STITCH
(over an odd number of sts)
ROW 1 (RS) K1, *p1, k1; rep from * to end.
ROW 2 K the purl sts and purl the knit sts.
Rep row 2 for seed st.

COWL
Cast on 49 sts. Work in seed st for 4 rows.
++BIND-OFF ROW (RS) Seed 4, [k2, pass first st over 2nd st to bind off 1 st, bind off 4 more sts, seed 3 (there are 4 sts from bind-off)] 5 times—5 bound-off sections with 4 sts seed in between.
SQUARE HOLE ROW (WS) Work 10 rows in seed st over first 4 sts on LH needle. Do not turn at end of last row.
***CAST-ON ROW (WS)** Cast on 6 sts onto RH needle using twisted loop cast-on.
Work 4 rows in seed st over next 4 sts *only* on LH needle. Turn work, bring yarn to back of work.
DROP ST AND CARRY-UP ROW (WS) Drop last cast-on st from RH needle, bring RH needle under the long loop of the dropped st, seed 1 from LH needle, then pass strand over st just worked on RH needle, seed 3, turn.

Work 3 rows in seed st over these 4 sts, turn, bring yarn to back of work.
CARRY-UP ROW (WS) Insert RH needle under same loose strand as before and seed 1 from LH needle, then pass strand over st just worked on RH needle, seed 3, turn.
Work 1 row seed st over these 4 sts, turn, bring yarn to back of work.
Work carry-up row once more—11 rows have been worked in the next seed 4 section.
Rep from * to end of row.
Work in seed st over all sts for 6 rows.
Rep from ++ for open squares pat 13 times more, ending with 4 rows of seed st instead of 6.
Bind off all sts in pat.

FINISHING
Sew cast-on and bound-off sts tog. ■

scarf quartet

A scarf is the perfect canvas for four different but equally striking combinations of color and texture.

Slip Stitch Checkered Scarf

■ ■ ■ ■

KNITTED MEASUREMENTS
Width 7"/18cm
Length 54"/137cm

MATERIALS
• 2 1¾oz/50g skeins (each approx 98yd/90m) of MountainTop by Classic Elite Yarns *Chalet* (baby alpaca/bamboo viscose) each in #7403 Light Gray (A) and #7477 Dark Gray (B) **⑤**

• One pair size 8 (5mm) needles OR SIZE TO OBTAIN GAUGE

GAUGE
18 sts and 28 rows = 4"/10cm over slip st pat using size 8 (5mm) needles.
TAKE TIME TO CHECK GAUGE.

SLIP STITCH PATTERN
(over a multiple of 4 sts plus 1)
ROW 1 (WS) With A, *k1, p1; rep from * to last st, k1.
ROWS 2 AND 4 K1B, *(p1, k1, p1)B, (sl 1 wyib); rep from * to last 4 sts, ([p1, k1] twice)B.
ROWS 3 AND 5 ([K1, p1] twice)B, *(sl 1 wyif), (p1, k1, p1)B; rep from * to last st, k1B.
ROWS 6 AND 8 With A, k1, *p1, k1; rep from * to end.
ROW 7 AND 9 With A, *k1, p1; rep from * to last st, k1.
Rep rows 2–9 for slip st pat.

SCARF
With A, cast on 33 sts.
Work in slip st pat until piece measures 54"/137cm from beg, ending with 2 rows A.
Bind off purlwise with A on RS. ■

Simple Striped Scarf

■ ■ ■ ■

KNITTED MEASUREMENTS
Width 8½"/21.5cm
Length 60"/152.5cm

MATERIALS
• 2 1¾oz/50g skeins (each approx 98yd/90m) of MountainTop by Classic Elite Yarns *Chalet* (baby alpaca/bamboo viscose) each in #7403 Light Gray (A) and #7477 Dark Gray (B) **⑤**

• One pair size 8 (5mm) needles OR SIZE TO OBTAIN GAUGE

GAUGE
18 sts and 28 rows = 4"/10cm over stripe pat using size 8 (5mm) needles. TAKE TIME TO CHECK GAUGE.

NOTE
The first and last 2 sts are worked in garter st (k every row) matching colors. These edge sts are included in the pattern stitch.

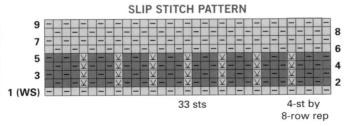

SLIP STITCH PATTERN

1 (WS)   33 sts   4-st by 8-row rep

● Design based on slip stitch checks on page 66.

STITCH KEY	COLOR KEY
☐ k on RS, p on WS	☐ Light Gray (A)
⊟ p on RS, k on WS	■ Dark Gray (B)
⩔ slip 1 wyib on RS, slip 1 wyif on WS	

scarf quartet

STRIPE PATTERN

(over a multiple of 4 sts plus 2)
ROW 1 (RS) With A, k2, *p2, k2; rep from * to end.
ROW 2 With A, k2, *k2, p2; rep from * to last 2 sts, end k2.
ROW 3 With B, k2, *k2, p2; rep from * to last 2 sts, end k2.
ROW 4 With B, k2, *p2, k2; rep from * to last 2 sts, end k2.
Rep rows 1–4 for stripe pat.

SCARF

With A, cast on 38 sts.
Work in stripe pat until piece measures approx 60"/152.5cm
from beg, ending with a pat row 2.
Bind off loosely in pat with A. ■

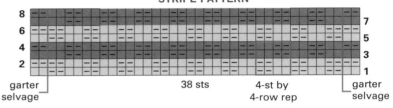

STRIPE PATTERN

garter selvage — 38 sts — 4-st by 4-row rep — garter selvage

Striped Moss Stitch Scarf
■ ■ ■ ■

KNITTED MEASUREMENTS
Width 7"/18cm
Length 70"/178cm

MATERIALS
• 3 1¾oz/50g skeins (each approx 98yd/90m) of
MountainTop by Classic Elite Yarns *Chalet* (baby alpaca/bamboo
viscose) in #7403 Light Gray (A)

• 1 skein in #7477 Dark Gray (B)

• One pair size 8 (5mm) needles OR SIZE TO OBTAIN GAUGE

GAUGE
20 sts and 24 rows = 4"/10cm over moss st using size 8
(5mm) needles. TAKE TIME TO CHECK GAUGE.

STRIPED MOSS STITCH

(over an odd number of sts)
ROW 1 (RS) With A, k1, *p1, k1; rep from * to end.
ROWS 2 AND 4 With A, k the knit sts and p the purl sts.
ROW 3 With A, p1, *k1, p1; rep from * to end.
ROWS 5 AND 6 Rep rows 1 and 2.
ROW 7 With B, p1, *k1, p1; rep from * to end.
ROW 8 With B, rep row 2.
Rep rows 1–8 for striped moss st.

NOTE
Carry yarn not in use loosely along side of work to avoid
cutting and weaving in ends.

SCARF
With A, cast on 35 sts.
Work in striped moss st until piece measures 70"/178cm
from beg, ending with a pat row 4.
Bind off purlwise with A on RS. ■

STRIPED MOSS STITCH

35 sts — 2-st by 4-row rep

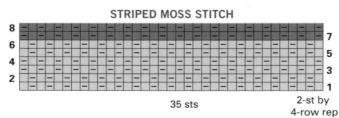

Vertical Striped Moss Stitch Scarf
■ ■ ■ ■

KNITTED MEASUREMENTS
Width 6"/15cm
Length 62"/157.5cm

MATERIALS
• 2 1¾oz/50g skeins (each approx 98yd/90m) of MountainTop
by Classic Elite Yarns *Chalet* (baby alpaca/bamboo viscose) each
in #7403 Light Gray (A) and #7477 Dark Gray (B) ⑤

• One pair size 8 (5mm) needles OR SIZE TO OBTAIN GAUGE

GAUGE
24 sts and 22 rows = 4"/10cm over vertical striped moss st
using size 8 (5mm) needles. TAKE TIME TO CHECK GAUGE.

VERTICAL STRIPED MOSS STITCH
(over an odd number of sts)
ROW 1 (RS) *K1A, p1B; rep from *, end k1A.
ROW 2 K the knit sts and p the purl sts, matching colors.
ROW 3 *P1A, k1B; rep from *, end p1A.
ROW 4 Rep row 2.
Rep rows 1–4 for vertical striped moss st.

SCARF
*With A, cast on 1 st, with B, cast on 1 st;
rep from * until 37 sts have been cast on.
Work in vertical striped moss st until piece measures approx
62"/157.5cm from beg, end with a pat row 4.
Bind off in pat, matching colors. ■

STITCH KEY	COLOR KEY
☐ k on RS, p on WS	☐ Light Gray (A)
⊟ p on RS, k on WS	■ Dark Gray (B)

● Design based on vertical
striped moss stitch on page 32.

VERTICAL STRIPED MOSS STITCH

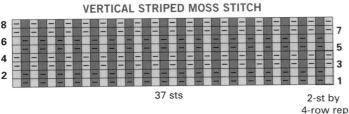

37 sts

2-st by
4-row rep

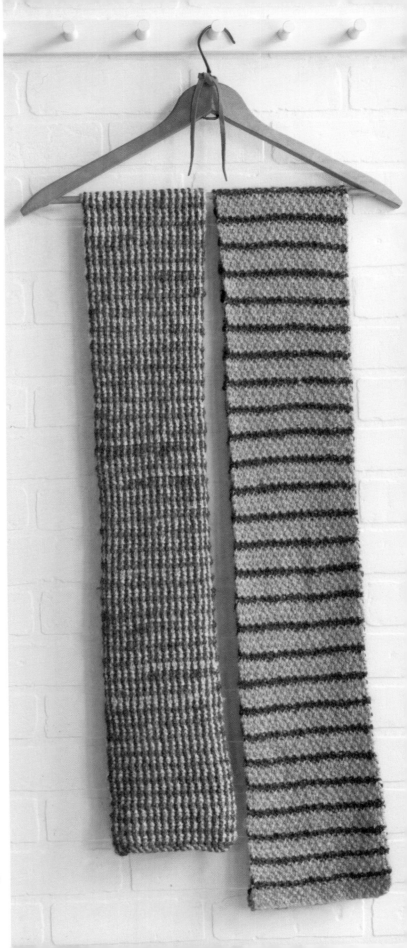

slip stitch bag

With checks on one side and stripes on the other, this bag looks lovely from any angle.

■ ■ ■ ■ ■

KNITTED MEASUREMENTS
Width 11"/28cm
Length 14"/35.5cm

MATERIALS
• 2 1¾oz/50g balls (each approx 155yd/140m) of Classic Elite Yarns *Firefly* (viscose/linen) in #7703 Silver (A) (2)

• 1 ball in #7788 Coral (B)

• One pair size 4 (3.5mm) needles OR SIZE TO OBTAIN GAUGE

• Two size 4 (3.5mm) double-pointed needles (dpn) for I-cord

GAUGE
21 sts and 42 rows = 4"/10cm over slip st pat
using size 4 (3.5mm) needles. TAKE TIME TO CHECK GAUGE.

NOTE
When working the stripes, carry color not in use loosely along side of work to avoid cutting and weaving in ends.

SLIP STITCH PATTERN
(over a multiple of 4 sts plus 1)
ROWS 1 AND 2 With A, *k1, p1; rep from *, end k1.
ROWS 3 AND 5 (RS) K1B, *(p1, k1, p1)B, (sl 1 wyib)A; rep from *

to last 4 sts, ([p1, k1] twice)B.
ROWS 4 AND 6 ([K1, p1] twice)B, *(sl 1 wyif)A, (p1, k1, p1)B; rep from * to last st, k1A.
ROWS 7 AND 8 With A, k1, *p1, k1; rep from * to end.
Rep rows 1–8 for slip st pat.

FRONT
With A, cast on 57 sts.
Work in slip st pat, working row 1–8 of pat 18 times, then work 2 more rows of seed st with A. Piece measures approx 14"/35.5cm from beg. Bind off in pat.

BACK
With A, cast on 57 sts. Work in seed st and stripe pat as foll:
*2 rows A, 4 rows B, 2 rows A; rep from * (8 rows) for stripe pat until there are the same number of rows as front, ending with 4 rows A. Bind off in pat with A.

FINISHING
Block lightly to measurements. Sew cast-on edges tog, then sew front and back tog along sides (matching stripes).

I-CORD STRAP
With dpn and A, cast on 5 sts.
***NEXT ROW (RS)** Knit. Do *not* turn. Slide sts back to beg of needle to work next row from RS; rep from * for I-cord until strap measures 24"/61cm or desired length. Bind off.
Sew ends of strap to inside of bag at each side seam. ■

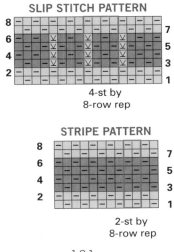

SLIP STITCH PATTERN

4-st by
8-row rep

STRIPE PATTERN

2-st by
8-row rep

STITCH KEY

☐ k on RS, p on WS

⊟ p on RS, k on WS

☑ slip 1 wyib on RS,
slip 1 wyif on WS

COLOR KEY

☐ Silver (A)

■ Coral (B)

● Design based on slip stitch checks on page 66.

zigzag poncho

Moss stitch is the backdrop for bands of chevron in a long poncho that exudes drama.

■ ■ ▨ ▨

SIZE
One size fits most.

MATERIALS
• 10 1¾oz/50g hanks (each approx 98yd/89m)
of Classic Elite Yarns *Chateau* (baby alpaca/bamboo viscose)
in #1458 crimson (5)

• Size 10½ (6.5mm) circular needle, 16"/40cm and 30"/76cm
long, OR SIZE TO OBTAIN GAUGE

• Stitch markers

• Stitch holders

KNITTED MEASUREMENTS
Width approx 35"/89cm
Length approx 25"/63.5cm

GAUGE
14 sts and 22 rows to 4"/10cm over moss stitch
using size 10½ (6.5mm) needles.
TAKE TIME TO CHECK YOUR GAUGE.

3-NEEDLE BIND-OFF
1. Hold right sides of pieces together on two needles.
Insert third needle knitwise into first st of each needle, and
wrap yarn knitwise.
2. Knit these two sts together, and slip them off the needles.
*Knit the next two sts together in the same manner.
3. Slip first st on 3rd needle over 2nd st and off needle.
Rep from * in step 2 across row until all sts are bound off.

MOSS STITCH
(over an odd number of sts)
ROW 1 (RS) *K1, p1; rep from * to last st, k1.
ROW 2 (WS) *P1, k1; rep from * to last st, p1.
ROW 3 *P1, k1; rep from * to last st, p1.
ROW 4 *K1, p1; rep from * to last st, k1.
Rep rows 1–4 for moss st.

SEED STITCH ZIGZAG
(multiple of 10 sts plus 1 and 15 rows)

ROW 1 (RS) *P1, k9; rep from * to last st, p1.
ROW 2 P1, *k1, p7, k1, p1; rep from * to end.
ROW 3 *P1, k1, p1, k5, p1, k1; rep from * to last st, p1.
ROW 4 P1, *k1, p1, k1, p3, [k1, p1] twice; rep from * to end.
ROW 5 *K2, [p1, k1] 4 times; rep from * to last st, k1.
ROW 6 P1, *p2, [k1, p1] twice, k1, p3; rep from * to end.
ROW 7 *K4, p1, k1, p1, k3; rep from * to last st, k1.
ROW 8 K1, *p4, k1; rep from * to end.
ROW 9 *K1, p1, k7, p1; rep from * to last st, k1.
ROW 10 K1, *p1, k1, p5, k1, p1, k1; rep from * to end.
ROW 11 *[K1, p1] twice, k3, p1, k1, p1; rep from * to last st, k1.
ROW 12 P1, *[p1, k1] 4 times, p2; rep from * to end.
ROW 13 *K3, [p1, k1] twice, p1, k2; rep from * to last st, k1.
ROW 14 P1, *p3, k1, p1, k1, p4; rep from * to end.
ROW 15 *K5, p1, k4; rep from * to last st, k1.

NOTE
A circular needle is used to accommodate the large number
of sts on the body. Do *not* join.

zigzag poncho

BACK
With longer circular needle, cast on 125 sts.
ROW 1 (RS) K2 (selvage sts), place marker (pm), work row 1 of moss st to last 2 sts, pm, k2 (selvage sts).
ROW 2 (WS) P2 (selvage sts), sl marker (sm), work row 2 of moss st to marker, sm, p2 (selvage sts).
Cont in pats as established, working moss st in between markers and 2 selvage sts each side in St st (k on RS, p on WS) until piece measures 5"/13cm from beg, end with a WS row.
Work 2 rows in St st.

BEG SEED ST ZIGZAG
ROW 1 (RS) K2 (selvage sts), sm, work row 2 of seed st zigzag to last 2 sts, sm, k2 (selvage sts).
Cont in pats as established through row 15 of seed st zigzag.
Purl 1 row, knit 1 row.
Work in moss st for 17 rows.
Knit 1 row, purl 1 row.
Work in seed st zigzag for 15 rows.
Purl 1 row, knit 1 row.
Beg with a WS row, work in moss st until piece measures 25"/63.5cm from beg, end with a WS row.
Place first 45 sts on one st holder for one shoulder, center 35 sts on 2nd holder for back neck and rem 45 sts on 3rd holder for 2nd shoulder.

FRONT
Work as for back until piece measures 22"/56cm from beg, end with a WS row.

SHAPE NECK
NEXT ROW (RS) Work 51 sts, place center 23 sts on holder for front neck, join second ball of yarn and work rem 51 sts.
Working both sides at once, bind off from each neck edge 3 sts once, 2 sts once, 1 st once.
Work even on rem 45 sts each side until piece measures same length as for back. Place sts each side on st holders.

FINISHING
Block pieces lightly to measurements. Join shoulders using 3-needle bind-off.

TURTLENECK
With RS facing and shorter circular needle, k 35 sts from back neck holder, pick up and k 13 sts along side of front neck, k 23 sts from front neck holder, pick up and k 13 sts along other side of front neck—84 sts. Join and place marker for beg of rnd. Work in k2, p2 rib for 4½"/11.5cm. Bind off loosely in rib. ■

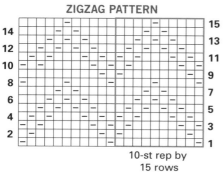

ZIGZAG PATTERN

14 12 10 8 6 4 2
15 13 11 9 7 5 3 1

10-st rep by
15 rows

STITCH KEY
☐ k on RS, p on WS
⊟ p on RS, k on WS

124

baby's crib blanket

A nubby organic cotton is great for baby and helps highlight different stitch patterns.

■■■■

KNITTED MEASUREMENTS
Approx 28 x 43"/71 x 109cm

MATERIALS
• 4 1¾oz/50g skeins (each approx 110yd/100m) of Verde Collection by Classic Elite Yarns *Sprout* (organic cotton) in #4301 White (A) ⑤

• 3 skeins in #4346 Green (B)

• Size 10 (6mm) circular needle, 32"/80cm long, OR SIZE TO OBTAIN GAUGE

GAUGE
13 sts and 18 rows = 4"/10cm over seed stitch using size 10 (6mm) needles.
TAKE TIME TO CHECK GAUGE.

NOTES
1. Keep first and last 5 sts in seed st with A.
2. Carry yarn not in use loosely along side of work to avoid cutting and weaving in ends.
3. When changing colors, twist yarns on WS to prevent holes.
4. Circular needle is used to accommodate the larger number of sts. Do *not* join.

SEED STITCH
(over an even number of sts)
ROW 1 (RS) *K1, p1; rep from * to end.
ROW 2 K the purl sts and p the knit sts.
Rep row 2 for seed st.

DOUBLE MOSS STITCH
(over a multiple of 4 sts)
ROW 1 (RS) *K2, p2; rep from * to end.
ROWS 2 AND 4 (WS) K the knit sts and p the purl sts.
ROW 3 *P2, k2; rep from * to end.
Rep rows 1–4 for double moss st.

125

baby's crib blanket

BLANKET
With A, cast on 90 sts.
*With A, work in seed st for 6 rows.
NEXT ROW (RS) (5 sts in seed st)A, join B and knit to last 5 sts, join 2nd ball of A, (5 sts in seed st)A.
NEXT ROW (WS) (5 sts in seed st)A, with B, purl to last 5 sts, (5 sts in seed st)A.
Rep from * once more.

BEG DOUBLE MOSS STITCH STRIPES
ROW 1 (RS) (5 sts in seed st)A, with A, work in double moss st to last 5 sts, (5 sts in seed st)A.
ROW 2 (WS) (5 sts in seed st)A, with A, work in double moss st to last 5 sts, (5 sts in seed st)A.
ROW 3 (5 sts in seed st)A, with B, work in double moss st to last 5 sts, (5 sts in seed st)A.
ROW 4 (WS) (5 sts in seed st)A, with B, work in double moss st to last 5 sts, (5 sts in seed st)A.
Rep rows 1–4 for double moss st stripes 9 times more (40 rows in total).
With A, knit 1 row, purl 1 row.

BEG SEED STITCH STRIPES
ROW 1 (RS) (5 sts in seed st)A, *p1A, k1B;
rep from * to last 5 sts, (5 sts in seed st)A.
ROW 2 (WS) (5 sts in seed st)A, *k1B, p1A;
rep from * to last 5 sts, (5 sts in seed st)A.
ROW 3 (5 sts in seed st)A, with A, *p1, k1;
rep from * to last 5 sts, (5 sts in seed st)A.
ROW 4 (5 sts in seed st)A, with A *k1, p1;
rep from * to last 5 sts, (5 sts in seed st)A.
Rep rows 1–4 for seed st stripes until piece measures approx 31"/78.5cm from beg, end with a pat row 2.

BEG DOUBLE MOSS STITCH STRIPES
Beg with row 3, work in double moss st stripes for 40 rows.
****NEXT ROW (RS)** (5 sts in seed st)A, with B, knit to last 5 sts, (5 sts in seed st)A.
NEXT ROW (WS) (5 sts in seed st)A, with B, purl to last 5 sts, (5 sts in seed st)A.
With A, work in seed st over all sts for 6 rows.
Rep from ** once more.
With A, bind off in pat.

FINISHING
Block lightly to measurements. ■

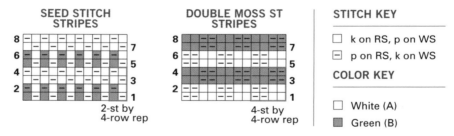

● Design based on horizontal striped double moss stitch on page 60.

eyelet baby blanket

Stripe with bold color and texture in a blanket that's cozy and delicate at the same time.

■■■■

KNITTED MEASUREMENTS
33 x 38"/84 x 96.5cm

MATERIALS
• 6 1¾oz/50g skeins (each approx 110yd/100m) of Classic Elite Yarns *Seedling* (organic cotton) in #4525 Pink (A) ④

• 3 skeins in #4501 White (B)

• Size 6 (4mm) circular needle, 32"/80cm long, OR SIZE TO OBTAIN GAUGE

• Stitch marker

GAUGE
15 sts and 30 rows = 4"/10cm over pat st using size 6 (4mm) needles.
TAKE TIME TO CHECK GAUGE.

NOTES
1. Keep first and last 6 sts in seed st with A.
2. Carry yarn not in use loosely along side inside edges of seed stitch border to avoid cutting and weaving in ends.

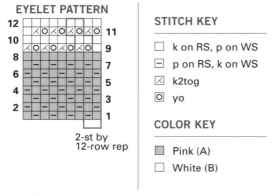

EYELET PATTERN

2-st by 12-row rep

STITCH KEY
☐ k on RS, p on WS
⊟ p on RS, k on WS
◺ k2tog
◎ yo

COLOR KEY
▨ Pink (A)
☐ White (B)

● Design based on eyelet stripes on page 36.

3. When changing colors, twist yarns on WS to prevent holes.
4. Circular needle is used to accommodate the large number of sts. Do *not* join.

SEED STITCH
(over an odd number of sts)
ROW 1 (RS) *K1, p1; rep from *, end k1.
Rep row 1 for seed st.

EYELET PATTERN
(over an odd number of sts)
ROWS 1–7 With A, *k1, p1; rep from * to end.
ROW 8 With A, purl.
ROW 9 With B, k1, *yo, k2tog; rep from * to end.
ROW 10 With B, purl.
ROW 11 With B, *yo, k2tog; rep from * to last st, k1.
ROW 12 Rep row 10.
Rep rows 1–12 for eyelet pat.

BLANKET
With A, cast on 125 sts.
Beg with k1, work in seed st for 2 rows.

BEG EYELET PATTERN
ROWS 1–7 With A, cont in seed st over all sts.
ROW 8 With A, work 6 sts in seed st, place marker (pm), purl to last 6 sts, pm, work 6 sts in seed st.
ROW 9 (6 sts seed st)A, slip marker (sm), with B, k1, *yo, k2tog; rep from * to last 6 sts, sm, join a 2nd ball of A and cont 6 sts in seed st.
ROW 10 (6 sts seed st)A, with B, purl to last 6 sts, (6 sts seed st)A.
ROW 11 (6 sts seed st)A, sm, with B, *yo, k2tog; rep from * to last 7 sts, k1B, sm, (6 sts seed st)A.
ROW 12 Rep row 10.

Cont in pats as established until rows 1–12 of eyelet pat have been worked 23 times. Cut B and 2nd ball of A.
With A, work in seed st over all sts for 8 rows. Bind off in pat.

FINISHING
Block lightly to measurements. ■

trio of baby hats

Cute, cuter, and cutest: any (or all!) of these
hats are a great quick gift for a little one.

■■■■

Vertical Striped Hat

SIZE
6–9 months

KNITTED MEASUREMENTS
Circumference 14½"/37cm
Height 7"/18cm (with edge unrolled)

MATERIALS
• 1 1¾oz/50g ball (each approx 136yd/125m) of Debbie Bliss/
KFI *Baby Cashmerino* (merino wool/acrylic/cashmere) each in
#340012 Silver (A) and #340086 Coral (B) **33**

• 1 pair size 3 (3.25mm) needles
OR SIZE TO OBTAIN GAUGE

• Yarn needle

GAUGE
26 sts and 36 rows = 4"/10cm over vertical stripe pat
using size 3 (3.25mm) needles.
TAKE TIME TO CHECK GAUGE.

NOTE
When changing colors, twist yarns on WS to prevent
holes in work. Carry yarn not in use loosely across
WS of work to prevent puckering.

SEED STITCH
(over an odd number of sts)
ROW 1 (RS) *K1, p1; rep from *, end k1.
Rep row 1 for seed st.

HAT
With A, cast on 95 sts. Work in St st (k on RS, p on WS)
for 10 rows. Join B.

BEG VERTICAL STRIPE PAT
ROW 1 (RS) [(P1, k1, p1)B, (k1, p1)A, (k1, p1, k1)B,
(p1, k1)A] 9 times, (p1, k1, p1)B, (k1, p1)A.
Cont in seed st and colors as established until piece
measures 5½"/14cm from beg, end with a WS row.

SHAPE CROWN
DEC ROW (RS) With B, *p3tog, with A, k1, p1, with B, k3tog,
with A, p1, k1; rep from *, end with A, k1, p1—57 sts.
Work even in seed st and colors as established for 3 rows.
DEC ROW (RS) *With B, p1, with A, k2tog; rep from * to end—38
sts. Cut B and cont with A to end of piece.
Purl 1 row.
DEC ROW (RS) *K2tog; rep from * to end—19 sts.
Purl 1 row.
Cut yarn, leaving a long tail. Thread through 19 sts twice,
pull tog tightly and secure end.

FINISHING
Sew back seam, reversing seam at beg 10 rows of St st so
that seam does not show on RS when edge is rolled. ■

**VERTICAL STRIPE
PATTERN**

STITCH KEY	COLOR KEY
☐ k on RS, p on WS	Silver (A)
⊟ p on RS, k on WS	Coral (B)

10-st by
6-row rep

● Design based on two-color vertical stripes on page 48.

trio of baby hats

Denim Striped Hat
■ ■ ■ ■

SIZE
6–9 months

KNITTED MEASUREMENTS
Circumference 14"/35.5cm
Height 6½"/16.5cm (with edge unrolled)

MATERIALS
• 1 1¾oz/50g ball (each approx 136yd/125m) of
Debbie Bliss/KFI *Baby Cashmerino* (merino wool/acrylic/cash-
mere) each in #340012 Silver (A) and #340027 Denim (B) ③

• 1 pair size 3 (3.25mm) needles
OR SIZE TO OBTAIN GAUGE

• Yarn needle

GAUGE
24 sts and 42 rows = 4"/10cm over stripe pat
using size 3 (3.25mm) needles.
TAKE TIME TO CHECK GAUGE.

NOTE
Carry yarn not in use loosely along side of work to avoid
cutting and weaving in ends.

SEED STITCH
(over an odd number of sts)
ROW 1 (RS) *K1, p1; rep from *, end k1.
Rep row 1 for seed st.

HAT
With A, cast on 85 sts. Work in St st (k on RS, p on WS)
for 10 rows. Join B.

BEG STRIPE PAT
ROWS 1–4 With B, *k1, p1; rep from *, end k1.
ROW 5 (RS) With A, knit.
ROW 6 (WS) With A, purl.
Rep rows 1–6 until 8 B stripes have been worked.

SHAPE CROWN
DEC ROW (RS) With A, *k1, k2tog tbl; rep from * to last st,
end k1—57 sts.
NEXT ROW Purl.
**NEXT ROW With B, work 4 rows in seed st.
DEC ROW With A, *k2tog tbl; rep from * to last st, k1—29 sts.
NEXT ROW With A, purl.**

Rep between **'s once more—15 sts.
Cut yarn, leaving a long tail. Thread through 15 sts twice,
pull tog tightly and secure end.

FINISHING
Sew back seam, reversing seam at beg 10 rows of St st so that
seam does not show on RS when edge is rolled. ■

Checkerboard Hat
■ ■ ■ ■

SIZE
6–9 months

KNITTED MEASUREMENTS
Circumference 14"/35.5cm
Height 7"/18cm (with edge unrolled)

MATERIALS
• 1 1¾oz/50g ball (each approx 136yd/125m) of
Debbie Bliss/KFI *Baby Cashmerino*
(merino wool/acrylic/cashmere) each in #340012 Silver (A),
#340086 Coral (B), and #340027 Denim (C) ③

• 1 pair size 3 (3.25mm) needles
OR SIZE TO OBTAIN GAUGE

• Yarn needle

GAUGE
24 sts and 42 rows = 4"/10cm over checkerboard pat
using size 3 (3.25mm) needles.
TAKE TIME TO CHECK GAUGE.

NOTE
When changing colors, twist yarns on WS to prevent
holes in work. Carry yarn not in use loosely across WS of
work to prevent puckering.

SEED STITCH
(over an even number of sts)
ROW 1 (RS) *K1, p1; rep from * to end.
ROW 2 (WS) *P1, k1; rep from * to end.
Rep rows 1 and 2 for seed st.

HAT
With A, cast on 85 sts. Work in St st (k on RS, p on WS) for 10
rows, dec 1 st at end of last WS row—84 sts. Join C.

STRIPE PATTERN

6								5
4								3
2								1

2-st by
6-row rep

STITCH KEY

☐ k on RS, p on WS

⊟ p on RS, k on WS

COLOR KEY

☐ Silver (A)

■ Denim (B)

● Design based on seed & stockinette stripes on page 62.

CHECKERBOARD PATTERN

12								11
10								9
8								7
6								5
4								3
2								1

6-st by
12-row rep

STITCH KEY

☐ k on RS, p on WS

⊟ p on RS, k on WS

COLOR KEY

☐ Silver (A)

■ Coral (B)

■ Denim (C)

● Design based on
checkerboard pattern on page 50.

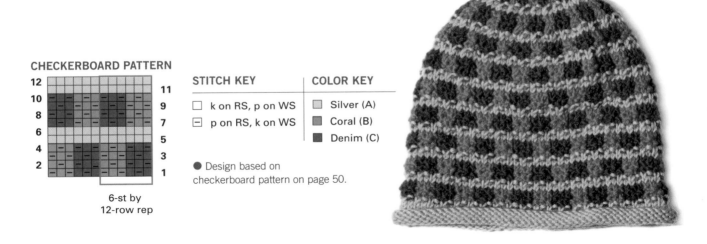

BEG CHECKERBOARD PAT
ROWS 1 AND 3 (RS) *(K1, p1, k1)C, (p1, k1, p1)B;
rep from * to end.
ROWS 2 AND 4 (WS) Work in seed st and colors as established.
ROWS 5 AND 6 With A, work in St st.
ROWS 7 AND 9 (RS) *(P1, k1, p1)B, (k1, p1, k1)C;
rep from * to end.
ROWS 8 AND 10 Work in seed st and colors as established.
ROWS 11 AND 12 With A, work in St st.
Rep rows 1–12 twice more, then rows 1–6 once.
Piece measures 5½"/14cm from beg, end with a WS row.

SHAPE CROWN
DEC ROW (RS) *With B, p1, k2tog, with C, p2tog, k1;
rep from * to end—56 sts.

Work even in seed st and colors as established for 3 rows.
With A, work in St st for 2 rows.
DEC ROW (RS) *With C, p2tog, with B, k2tog;
rep from * to end—28 sts.
Work even in seed st and colors as established for 3 rows.
Cut B and C.
Cont with A to end of piece.
Knit 1 row.
DEC ROW (WS) *P2tog; rep from * to end—14 sts.
Cut yarn, leaving a long tail. Thread through 14 sts twice,
pull tog tightly and secure end.

FINISHING
Sew back seam, reversing seam at beg 10 rows of St st so that
seam does not show on RS when edge is rolled. ■

girl's & boy's baby cardis

Details make the difference in two distinct looks with the same basic shape.

Baby Girl's Cardi (left)
■ ■ ▨ ▨

SIZES
6–9 (9–12, 12–18) months

KNITTED MEASUREMENTS
Chest 23 (24, 25½)"/58.5 (61, 64.5)cm
Length 10 (10½, 11½)"/25.5 (26.5, 29)cm

MATERIALS
• 2 1¾oz/50g balls (each approx 136yd/125m) of Debbie Bliss/KFI *Baby Cashmerino* (merino wool/acrylic/cashmere) in #340086 Coral (A)

• 1 ball in #340012 Silver (B)

• 1 pair size 4 (3.5mm) needles OR SIZE TO OBTAIN GAUGE

• Size E/4 (3.5mm) crochet hook

• Two ¾"/20mm buttons

• Yarn needle

GAUGE
26 sts and 28 rows = 4"/10cm over stripe pat
using size 4 (3.5mm) needles. TAKE TIME TO CHECK GAUGE.

NOTES
1. Cardigan is worked in one piece, from the lower edge of the fronts to the lower edge of the back.
2. When working in stripe pat, carry yarn not in use loosely along side of work to avoid cutting and weaving in ends.

STRIPE PATTERN
(over an odd number of sts)
ROW 1 (RS) With A, k1, *p1, k1; rep from * to end.
ROW 2 With A, k the knit sts and p the purl sts.

ROW 3 P1A, *k1B, p1A; rep from * to end.
ROW 4 K the knit sts and p the purl sts, matching colors.
Rep rows 1–4 for stripe pat.

LEFT FRONT
With A, cast on 37 (39, 41) sts.
Rep rows 1–4 of stripe pat for a total of 40 (44, 48) rows—piece measures approx 5½ (6, 6½)"/14 (15.5, 16.5)cm from beg, ending with a pat row 4.

SLEEVE
ROW 1 (RS) With A, cast on 26 (28, 30) sts, k1, *p1, k1; rep from * to end—63 (67, 71) sts.
ROW 2 With A, k the knit sts and p the purl sts.
Beg with row 3, cont in stripe pat as established until a total of 61 (65, 69) rows have been worked from beg, piece measures approx 8 ½ (9, 10)"/21.5 (23, 25.5)cm from beg, end with a pat row 1.

NECK SHAPING
NEXT ROW (WS) Bind off 5 (5, 6) sts (neck edge), work to end. Cont to bind off from neck edge 3 sts twice, 2 sts once—50 (54, 57) sts.
Work even until a total of 71 (75, 83) rows have been worked from beg, ending with pat row 3. Place a marker at sleeve edge to mark center of piece. Place sts on a holder.

RIGHT FRONT
Work to correspond to left front, reversing sleeve and neck shaping.

BACK
JOINING ROW (WS) Beg with row 4, cont in stripe pat and work 50 (54, 57) sts from left front holder, cast on 27 sts, work 50 (54, 57) sts from right front holder—127 (135, 141) sts.
Work even in stripe pat until a total of 31 (31, 35) rows have been worked from center markers.
Bind off 26 (28, 30) sts at beg of next 2 rows—75 (79, 81) sts.
Work even in stripe pat until a total of 71 (75, 83) rows have been worked from center markers, end with a pat row 2.
Bind off in pat with A.

STRIPE PATTERN

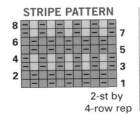

2-st by
4-row rep

STITCH KEY	COLOR KEY
☐ k on RS, p on WS	▨ Coral (A)
⊟ p on RS, k on WS	☐ Silver (B)

● Design based on two-row striped moss stitch on page 58.

girl's and boy's baby cardis

SLEEVE CUFFS

With RS facing and A, pick up and k 39 (39, 43) sts evenly along sleeve edge. Work in k1, p1 rib as foll:
NEXT ROW (WS) *P1, k1; rep from *, end p1.
NEXT ROW K1, *p1, k1; rep from * to end. Bind off in rib.

FINISHING
Block lightly to measurements. Sew side and sleeve seams.

EDGING
With RS facing, crochet hook and A, beg at lower right front edge, work sc evenly along right front edge until 2½"/6.5cm before first neck bind-off, ch 4, skip ½"/1.5cm (for button loop), work 4 sc along edge, ch 4, skip ½"/1.5cm (for button loop), then cont sc around evenly around rem right front edge and work 3 sc in corner of neck, along back neck, and then along left front edge, working 3 sc in corner of neck, end at lower left front edge. Fasten off. Sew on buttons. ∎

Baby Boy's Cardi (lower left)
■ ■ ▪ ▪

SIZES
6–9 (9–12, 12–18) months

KNITTED MEASUREMENTS
Chest 23 (24, 25½)"/58.5 (61, 64.5)cm
Length 10 (10½, 11½)"/25.5 (26.5, 29)cm

MATERIALS
• 3 1¾oz/50g balls (each approx 136yd/125m)
of Debbie Bliss/KFI *Baby Cashmerino*
(merino wool/acrylic/cashmere) in #34009 Slate (A) ⟨3⟩

• 2 balls in #340012 Silver (B)

• 1 pair size 4 (3.5mm) needles OR SIZE TO OBTAIN GAUGE

• Size E/4 (3.5mm) crochet hook

• Two ¾"/20mm buttons

• Yarn needle

GAUGE
24 sts and 48 rows = 4"/10cm over seed st
using size 4 (3.5mm) needles. TAKE TIME TO CHECK GAUGE.

NOTES
1. Cardigan is worked in one piece, from the lower edge

of the fronts to the lower edge of the back.

2. When working in stripe pat, carry yarn not in use loosely along side of work to avoid cutting and weaving in ends.

SEED STITCH
(over an odd number of sts)
ROW 1 (RS) *K1, p1; rep from *, end k1.
Rep row 1 for seed st.

LEFT FRONT
With A, cast on 35 (37, 39) sts.
Work in seed st for 6 (6, 8) rows. Join B.

BEG STRIPE PAT
*With B, work 4 rows in seed st. With A, work 4 rows in seed st; rep from * (8 rows) for stripe pat until 66 (74, 76) rows have been worked from beg, ending with 4 rows B—piece measures approx 5½ (6, 6½)"/14 (15.5, 16.5)cm.

SLEEVE
NEXT ROW (RS) With A, cast on 36 (38, 40) sts, work seed st to end—71 (75, 79) sts.
Cont in seed st and stripe pat until 109 (117, 127) rows have been worked from beg, ending with 3 rows A—piece measures approx 9 (9 ½, 10)"/23 (24.5, 25.5)cm from beg.

NECK SHAPING
NECK EDGE (WS) Bind off 5 (5, 6) sts (neck edge), work to end. Cont to bind off from neck edge 3 sts twice, 2 sts once—58 (62, 65) sts.
Work even until a total of 120 (128, 138) rows have been worked from beg, ending with 2 rows B. Place a marker at sleeve edge to mark center of piece. Place sts on a holder.

RIGHT FRONT
Work to correspond to left front, reversing sleeve and neck shaping.

BACK
JOINING ROW (RS) Cont stripe pat, work 58 (62, 65) sts from right front holder, cast on 25 sts, work 58 (62, 65) sts from left front holder—141 (149, 155) sts.
Work even in stripe pat until there are 54 (54, 62) rows from center markers.
Bind off 36 (38, 40) sts at beg of next 2 rows—69 (73, 75) sts.
Work even in stripe pat until there are 114 (122, 130) rows from center markers, ending with 4 rows B.
With A, work 6 (6, 8) rows in seed st. Bind off in pat with A.

SLEEVE CUFFS
With RS facing, crochet hook and A, work 1 row sc evenly

along each sleeve edge. Fasten off.

FINISHING
Block lightly to measurements. Sew side and sleeve seams, sewing 1½"/4cm at lower edge of sleeve on WS for turning cuff back.

OUTER BODY EDGING
With WS facing, crochet hook and A, beg at lower left front edge, work 1 row sc evenly along left front edge, working 3 sc in corner of neck at first neck bind-off, along back neck, and along right front edge, working 3 sc in corner of neck as before, ending at lower right front edge. Fasten off.

BUTTON LOOPS
With RS facing, join yarn to left front neck edge just below the 3-sc corner, ch 4, skip ½"/1.5cm, work 4 sc along edge, ch 4, skip ½"/1.5cm, then join yarn in next st and fasten off.
Sew on buttons.

POCKET
With B, cast on 15 sts. Work in seed st for 1½"/4cm.
Change to A and cont in seed st for 3 rows. Bind off in pat.
Sew pocket to left front (see photo) or where desired. ∎

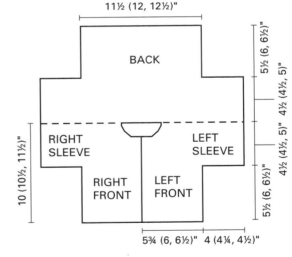

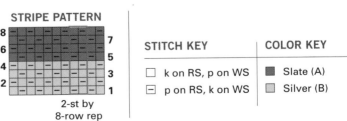

STITCH KEY		COLOR KEY	
□	k on RS, p on WS	■	Slate (A)
⊟	p on RS, k on WS	□	Silver (B)

2-st by 8-row rep

● Design based on two-row striped seed stitch on page 58.

things to know

ABBREVIATIONS

approx	approximately
beg	begin(ning)
CC	contrasting color
ch	chain
cm	centimeter(s)
cn	cable needle
cont	continu(e)(ing)
dc	double crochet
dec	decreas(e)(ing)
dpn	double-pointed needle(s)
foll	follow(s)(ing)
g	gram(s)
inc	increas(e)(ing)
k	knit
kfb	knit into the front and back of a stitch—one stitch is increased
k2tog	knit 2 stitches together
LH	left-hand
lp(s)	loop(s)
m	meter(s)
M1	make 1 (knit st) by inserting tip of LH needle from front to back under the strand between the last stitch and the next stitch; knit into the back loop

M1 p-st	make 1 purl stitch
MC	main color
mm	millimeter(s)
oz	ounce(s)
p	purl
p2tog	purl 2 stitches together
pat(s)	pattern(s)
pm	place maker
psso	pass slip stitch(es) over
rem	remain(s)(ing)
rep	repeat
RH	right-hand
rnd(s)	round(s)
RS	right side(s)
S2KP	slip 2 sts together knit 1, pass 2 slip stitches over knit 1
sc	single crochet
SKP	slip 1, knit 2, pass slip stitch over
SK2P	slip 1, knit 2, together, pass slip stitch over the knit 2 together
sl	slip
sl st	slip stitch
sm	slip marker

ssk (ssp)	slip next 2 stitches knitwise (purlwise) one at a time; knit (purl) these 2 stitches tog
sssk	slip next 3 stitches knitwise, one at a time, knit these 3 stitches together
st(s)	stitch(es)
St st	stockinette stitch
tbl	through back loop(s)
tog	together
tr	treble crochet
WS	wrong side(s)
wyib	with yarn in back
wyif	with yarn in front
yd	yard(s)
yo	yarn over needle
*	repeat directions following * as many times as indicated
[]	repeat directions inside brackets as many times as indicated

KNITTING NEEDLES

U.S.	METRIC
0	2mm
1	2.25mm
2	2.75mm
3	3.25mm
4	3.5mm
5	3.75mm
6	4mm
7	4.5mm
8	5mm
9	5.5mm
10	6mm
10½	6.5mm
11	8mm
13	9mm
15	10mm
17	12.75mm
19	15mm
35	19mm

FOLLOWING THE CHARTS

Some of the stitch patterns in this book begin on a wrong-side row and therefore you work the first rows of the chart by reading from the left to the right. It is sometimes harder to follow the symbols on the wrong-side rows, as you work them in the opposite way as they appear on the chart. That is, the blank square will be a purl stitch and the dash (–) symbol will be worked as a knit stitch.

standard yarn weight system

CATEGORIES OF YARN, GAUGE RANGES, AND RECOMMENDED NEEDLE AND HOOK SIZES

Yarn Weight Symbol & Category	0 Lace	1 Super Fine	2 Fine	3 Light	4 Medium	5 Bulky	6 Super Bulky	7 Jumbo
Type of Yarns in Category	Fingering 10-count crochet thread	Sock, Fingering, Baby	Sport, Baby	DK, Light Worsted	Worsted, Afghan, Aran	Chunky, Craft, Rug	Super Bulky, Roving	Jumbo, Roving
Knit Gauge Range* in Stockinette Stitch to 4 inches	33–40** sts	27–32 sts	23–26 sts	21–24 sts	16–20 sts	12–15 sts	7–11 sts	6 sts and fewer
Recommended Needle in Metric Size Range	1.5–2.25 mm	2.25—3.25 mm	3.25—3.75 mm	3.75—4.5 mm	4.5—5.5 mm	5.5—8 mm	8—12.75 mm	12.75 mm and larger
Recommended Needle U.S. Size Range	000–1	1 to 3	3 to 5	5 to 7	7 to 9	9 to 11	11 to 17	17 and larger
Crochet Gauge* Ranges in Single Crochet to 4 inch	32–42 double crochets**	21–32 sts	16–20 sts	12–17 sts	11–14 sts	8–11 sts	6–9 sts	5 sts and fewer
Recommended Hook in Metric Size Range	Steel*** 1.6–1.4 mm	2.25—3.5 mm	3.5—4.5 mm	4.5—5.5 mm	5.5—6.5 mm	6.5—9 mm	9—16 mm	16 mm and larger
Recommended Hook U.S. Size Range	Steel*** 6, 7, 8 Regular hook B–1	B–1 to E–4	E–4 to 7	7 to I–9	I–9 to K–10 1/2	K–10 1/2 to M–13	M–13 to Q	Q and larger

* GUIDELINES ONLY: The above reflect the most commonly used gauges and needle or hook sizes for specific yarn categories.

** Lace weight yarns are usually knitted or crocheted on larger needles and hooks to create lacy, openwork patterns. Accordingly, a gauge range is difficult to determine. Always follow the gauge stated in your pattern.

*** Steel crochet hooks are sized differently from regular hooks—the higher the number, the smaller the hook, which is the reverse of regular hook sizing

This Standards & Guidelines booklet and downloadable symbol artwork are available at: **YarnStandards.com**

SKILL LEVELS

■ ▪ ▪ ▪
BEGINNER
IDEAL FIRST PROJECT.

■ ■ ▪ ▪
EASY
BASIC STITCHES, MINIMAL SHAPING, AND SIMPLE FINISHING.

■ ■ ■ ▪
INTERMEDIATE
FOR KNITTERS WITH SOME EXPERIENCE. MORE INTRICATE STITCHES, COLOR-WORK AND CHART READING.

■ ■ ■ ■
EXPERIENCED
FOR KNITTERS ABLE TO WORK PATTERNS WITH COMPLICATED SHAPING AND FINISHING.

index

resources

CASCADE YARNS
cascadeyarns.com

CLASSIC ELITE YARNS
classiceliteyarns.com

DEBBIE BLISS/KFI
knittingfever.com/brand/debbie-bliss/yarn

FIBRA NATURA/UNIVERSAL YARNS
universalyarn.com

FYBERSPATES
fyberspates.com

LONG ISLAND LIVESTOCK CO.
lilivestockco.com

MANOS DEL URUGUAY/ FAIRMOUNT FIBERS
fairmountfibers.com

NORO/KFI
knittingfever.com/brand/noro/yarn

ROWAN
knitrowan.com

TAHKI YARNS/TAHKI•STACY CHARLES
tahkistacycharles.com

YARNS USED IN SWATCHES

Cashmerino Aran from Debbie Bliss/ KFI: pp. 18–67

220 Superwash from Cascade Yarns: p. 68 (top)

Euroflax from Louet North America: p. 68 (bottom)

Rhapsody from ArtYarns: p. 70 (top)

Silk Garden from Noro: p. 70 (bottom)

Angel from Debbie Bliss/KFI: p. 72 (top and bottom)

220 Superwash from Cascade Yarns: p. 72 (top and bottom)

Silky Merino from Malabrigo: pp. 74 (top and bottom), 76 (top)

Zarina from Tahki•Stacy Charles: p. 76 (bottom)

Shiraito from Noro: p. 76 (bottom)

 104 W 27th St, 3rd Floor, New York, NY 10001

www.sixthandspring.com

Editor
LISA SILVERMAN

Associate Editor
JACOB SEIFERT

Art Director
DIANE LAMPHRON

Yarn Editor
JACLENE SINI

Supervising Patterns Editor
CARLA SCOTT

Technical Illustrator
LORETTA DACHMAN

Stylist
JOSEFINA GARCIA

Hair and Makeup
NICKEE DAVID

Vice President/ Editorial Director
TRISHA MALCOLM

Vice President/ Publisher
CAROLINE KILMER

Production Manager
DAVID JOINNIDES

President
ART JOINNIDES

Chairman
JAY STEIN

PHOTOGRAPHY CREDITS
Jack Deutsch:
pp. 3, 7, 9, 10–11, 15–17, 78–79, 90, 116, 119, 120, 125–130, 134–137, 143
Marcus Tullis:
pp. 8, 13–14, 18–77, 91, 98, 117–118, 119, 121, 131–133
Rose Callahan:
pp. 80–89, 92–97, 100–115, 122–124

acknowledgments

This book could not be possible without the incredible support and encouragement from so many people. I'd like to thank the staff at Soho Publishing and Sixth&Spring Books: Art Joinnides, for giving me the wonderful opportunity to explore seed stitch; Trisha Malcolm, whose humor and unwavering support brought me through the thick and thin of it; Carla Scott, for whom I have the deepest appreciation, as without her amazing technical expertise and dearest friendship, this book could not have happened. I would like to thank Loretta Dachman for creating such clear charts, Lisa Silverman for her editing expertise, Diane Lamphron for designing the book, and Jacob Seifert and Joan Krellenstein for their work behind the scenes. Special thanks Cornelia Tuttle Hamilton to Kathleen Kennedy, Harriett Elliott, Annabelle Speer, and Hannah Wallace for their knitting contributions. Much appreciation also goes to the many yarn companies who generously contributed the beautiful yarns you see throughout the book, to the talented photographers who make my work look so good, and to anyone else I may have forgotten. It's been a pleasure and a joy to write this book, and I hope you enjoy your own personal exploration of my favorite stitch!

about the author

ROSEMARY DRYSDALE is a designer and teacher of knitting and embroidery. Growing up in Northern England, she learned to knit socks at age seven and was introduced to embroidery by her grandmother. Rosemary studied textile science in college, earning a distinction in needlework studies. After relocating to the United States in her early twenties, she enjoyed a decades-spanning career as an embroidery and knitting teacher and designer at Pratt Institute and FIT in New York. She's traveled the world lecturing and promoting her publications. More recently, she was a yarn store owner and is currently Knitting Editor at *Vogue®Knitting* and *Knit Simple* magazines. She is also a consultant in the yarn industry and designer for numerous publications, as well as Tahki•Stacy Charles. Rosemary's books include the bestselling *Entrelac* and *Entrelac 2*.

116

100

120

134

107

86

94